Reading
Upside Down

Reading Upside Down

Identifying and Addressing Opportunity Gaps in Literacy Instruction

Deborah L. Wolter

Foreword by
Richard L. Allington

TEACHERS COLLEGE PRESS

TEACHERS COLLEGE | COLUMBIA UNIVERSITY
NEW YORK AND LONDON

Published by Teachers College Press, 1234 Amsterdam Avenue, New York, NY 10027

Library of Congress Cataloging-in-Publication Data is available at loc.gov

ISBN 978-0-8077-5665-2 (paperback)
ISBN 978-0-8077-5666-9 (hardcover)
ISBN 978-0-8077-7385-7 (ebook)

Printed on acid-free paper
Manufactured in the United States of America

22 21 20 19 18 17 16 15   8 7 6 5 4 3 2 1

Contents

Foreword

Deborah L. Wolter has written a powerful argument for reconsidering the etiology of the reading difficulties that too many children experience in American schools. In *Reading Upside Down* you will find an engaging discussion of why we must begin to ask questions of a very different type from those questions we have typically asked when we attempt to explain the reading difficulties that some children experience.

This book raises the questions we need to be asking ourselves whenever we encounter children struggling while learning to read, the key one being whether the observed reading difficulties are a result of instruction that is too inexpert and too inadequate to result in developing the literacy proficiency of the struggling readers. This question, which is too rarely considered, is actually a research-base done. Note what Vellutino and Fletcher (2005), two experienced researchers who have had their studies of children identified as learning disabled or dyslexic funded by the National Institutes for Health, wrote recently after reviewing the research on the underlying causes of learning disabilities and dyslexia:

> Finally, there is now considerable evidence, from recent intervention studies, that reading difficulties in most beginning readers may not be directly caused by biologically based cognitive deficits intrinsic to the child, but may in fact be related to the *opportunities* provided for children learning to read (emphasis added). (p. 378)

In other words, they identify the problems of struggling readers primarily as a lack of access to expert instruction coupled with too limited opportunities to read. What their studies, and others, have demonstrated is that virtually all children entering kindergarten could be reading well by the end of 1st grade!

However, few schools provide the sort of expert and intensive reading instruction that some children need to succeed as readers. Even fewer schools provide the 30–60 hours of high-quality professional development necessary to develop primary-grade teachers' expertise sufficiently

(McGill-Franzen, Allington, Yokoi, & Brooks, 1999; Scanlon, Gelzheiser, Vellutino, Schatschneider, & Sweeney, 2008). What most struggling beginning readers get as additional support in learning to read, if anything at all, is daily time to work with a paraprofessional or community volunteer. But it is rare to find an adult in either of these two categories who is considered expert in their ability to provide powerful literacy lessons. Too often, after experiencing an ineffective intervention, these children become candidates for retention in grade or for special education services (Allington, 2012).

However, when schools are organized such that struggling early readers have access to larger amounts of expert literacy lessons each day, the number of students who continue to struggle with reading drops dramatically. So too do the numbers of children who experience being retained in grade or labeled as needing special education services.

Children enter kindergarten with diverse experiences with reading and writing, as well as come to school from diverse home language environments. What this means for every kindergarten teacher is that children will differ in important ways when it comes to planning appropriate instruction. It also means that commercial one-size-fits-all curriculum materials simply will not offer teachers or students a flexible enough framework to ensure every child becomes a reader. We know how to create classrooms where all children become readers, but instead, in most schools, we continue to label children as "ready" or "unready" for school and offer them little in the way of expert and intensive reading instruction.

In the end, Deborah L. Wolter demonstrates the powerful negative effects our persistent belief that children somehow will benefit from being labeled and provided instructional support somewhere outside the classroom by someone other than the child's assigned classroom teacher. She demonstrates through the effective use of short case studies how children are typically "helped," as well as an alternative, effective and personalized reading instruction that might be provided instead to turn struggling readers into achieving readers.

It is this hopeful stance that makes me so appreciate this book. The book not only challenges the status quo but offers a rationale alternative that would benefit every struggling reader. I hope *Reading Upside Down* initiates a widespread movement to undo so much of what we have done in the name of "helping" children who struggle with learning to read. We now know enough to create much better options for children and for their teachers. It is damn well time to begin the changes that are absolutely necessary, and *Reading Upside Down* provides the essential elements of the plan that educators need to implement.

So, my advice is this: Read this book and then begin developing an instructional plan that will lead to the elimination of the struggles some children now face as we begin their journey to becoming literate.

Richard L. Allington

REFERENCES

Allington, R. L. (2012). *What really matters for struggling readers: Designing research-based programs* (3rd ed.). Boston, M. A.: Pearson-Allyn-Bacon.

McGill-Franzen, A., Allington, R. L., Yokoi, L., & Brooks, G. (1999). Putting books in the classroom seems necessary but not sufficient. *Journal of Educational Research, 93*(2), 67–74.

Scanlon, D. M., Gelzheiser, L. M., Vellutino, F. R., Schatschneider, C., & Sweeney, J. M. (2008). Reducing the incidence of early reading difficulties: Professional development for classroom teachers versus direct interventions for children. *Learning and Individual Differences, 18*(3), 346–359.

Vellutino, F. R., & Fletcher, J. M. (2005). Developmental dyslexia. In M. Snowling & C. Hulme (Eds.), *The science of reading: A handbook* (pp. 362–378). Malden, MA: Blackwell.

Acknowledgments

To my childhood school principal, the late Dr. David Aberdeen, his cadre of devoted teachers, and my parents, I am eternally grateful for my opportunity for an education.

To my administrators and colleagues, even those who felt skeptical at first, thank you for accepting, trusting, and collaborating with me as a professional throughout my career.

Not only does it take a community to raise and educate a child and run schools, it takes many to bring up a book for publication. Thank you to those who provided encouragement and guidance along the way: Jeannie Ballew, who coached me from the beginning; Emily Spangler, who saw its strength and guided me in cultivating it more fully for publication; Philip Zazove, who knows the world of deafness and what writing a book (or two) entails; Aureliano Vazquez, who oversaw the production process of my manuscript to its final printing; and many reviewers and friends who provided valuable insights and moral support, large and small. And much love to my husband, Klaus, and my two children, Keane and Kara, for their enduring faith and gentle support.

To my students and their families over the years, thank you for exploring our languages and literacies with me as we all strived to move from *reading upside down* to *reading right side up*. This book is for you and your children.

Reading Upside Down

JENNA

Many children learn to read and write naturally, fluently, and without any difficulties, many even as preschoolers before formal schooling. Parents are immensely proud and teachers are pleased. These children usually come from environments that support literacy. They have an abundance of children's books, are frequently read aloud to, and make regular trips to the library. They enjoy the warm, personal interactions with adults that bedtime stories bring. They have plenty of paper and other materials on which to scribble, invent, spell, and draw. Chalk on the sidewalk, magnetic letters on the refrigerator, and letter-shaped bath sponges are a common part of their young lives. Eventually, they begin to recognize text patterns, try to read and write on their own, and generally start off on a path toward educational achievement.

Jenna, however, was brought to my attention in my role as a teacher consultant. In 4th grade and already qualified for special education, she still had not learned to read fluently past a kindergarten level. Her teachers were concerned and her parents became angry. When I asked Jenna's teacher and special education teacher, both of whom were very well meaning and kind, what was going on—why she hadn't learned to read—I received many answers. I was told Jenna had been a "late bloomer" by the time she arrived in kindergarten. Requesting more specifics, I asked how that impacted her learning to read in school now that she was in 4th grade. Brushing my question off, I was told she had been diagnosed with attention deficit disorder (ADD). So again, I gently questioned how that specifically impacted her learning to read. Many students with ADD learn how to read. From there, I was told that she had overbearing parents. Again, how would that impact her learning to read? Finally, I was told that she was tall for her age and that that affected her self-esteem. By this time, I had heard enough. It became clear that I would have to do some observations and diagnostics of Jenna's attempts at reading so I could find out for myself . . . and for Jenna, just what was at the heart of her lack of reading skills.

Jenna's strengths were evident right away. She had strong language ability in that she was able to carry on a conversation and tell stories, and she had an excellent core of vocabulary words. Jenna also had a wealth of background knowledge; her parents frequently took her to the zoo, science museum, the library, and on family trips. In addition, she was read aloud to each night and knew many classic stories. At school, she listened to her teacher read chapter books aloud and eagerly looked forward to the next day's segment.

Alas, Jenna was not reading much on her own and she even announced to me during our first session together that she has dyslexia. At least that was what she was told by her parents. It turned out that Jenna was primarily a visual reader at the cost of using structural and semantic cues. She thought she had to sound out each word before moving on to the next word. She struggled to remember all the phonetic "rules," such as the concept that a silent /e/ makes a vowel long or that a /c/ can sound like an /s/ and a /y/ can sound like an /i/ or an /e/ in some words. In attempting to read the word *definitely*, she couldn't remember how the syllables were to be divided: *def / in / it / ely, de / fin / ite / ly*, or *def / in / i / tel / ly*. She was so focused on letters and words that she lost all meaning. In special education, she had been exclusively taught phonics as a method for learning to read, one letter and one rule at a time. As she made her way through the phonics program, she forgot the prior lessons from weeks before. Yet at the same time, she did not have enough practice reading real books, using other strategies involving structural and semantic cues, to compensate for her weakness in phonological processing. This, in turn, didn't help her become proficient and fluent in reading letters and words. On top of that, because reading was such an arduous process for her, her attention wavered. Her parents turned out to be "overbearing," in the words of her teachers, only because they were rightfully concerned about her and questioned the school's ability to teach her to read. And yes, she was tall for her age, but her self-esteem was probably more affected by her feeling frustrated and unable to keep up with her class.

Jenna missed a crucial opportunity to learn to read in her early elementary years. Because she was developmentally delayed in kindergarten, she was placed in a special education program. Ever since then, she had been bogged down with having to learn phonics in isolation. Unfortunately, phonological processing was her weakest link in reading, but also the one that received the most focus in special education reading instruction. There was little recognition of her strengths or the fact that she would have benefited more from learning other reading strategies such as using structural and semantic cues for decoding unknown words. Instead, because Jenna had very low scores on district and state tests year after year, she stayed on with a "specialized" reading program that ultimately didn't work for her. When I met her, she had spent the previous year attempting to learn to read using an online reading program, which, unfortunately, had a similar emphasis on phonics, one letter and one rule at a time.

By 4th grade, Jenna began to cry uncontrollably and frequently at school. Her teachers and principal were alarmed, as she had always been a dutiful, seemingly happy child. Her parents were beside themselves with worry, a psychologist was consulted, and the district administrator called me in. After reviewing Jenna's history and doing several assessments of her reading, I started teaching her how to read in purposeful ways using real books—a different approach from the phonics-based instruction that she'd been getting through special education reading programs. In 3 months' time, Jenna made an entire year's worth of growth. She started reading picture books to her baby brother and the family dog at home, which brought tears to her parents' eyes. In another 3 months' time, she started reading chapter books with her best friend. And slowly, she started to feel better about school.

Unfortunately, there are many students like Jenna. These are the students who are delayed in learning to read and write because they:

- were unready for kindergarten;
- were not adequately taught how to read in kindergarten through 3rd grade;
- have a medically identified disability;
- speak another language instead of or in addition to English;
- speak a variation of English, such as African American English;
- have a speech and language disorder;
- have Black or Brown skin;
- were reluctant or otherwise misbehaving students
- are impoverished or homeless;
- have parents who prefer not to become involved with a formal schooling context or lack academic literacy; or
- were subjected to standardized tests with dubious results for high-stakes decisionmaking.

Although these circumstances are totally beyond their control, absolutely none of them should be an excuse for students' failure to learn to read and write in a timely manner. The current structure of the educational system allows teachers, administrators, and even parents to focus on what is *wrong* with students and is concerned with how they *can't* or *won't* learn to read and write with well-developed strategies and fluency. Instead, educators—particularly general education teachers—are in a prime position to shift from a viewpoint of deficits in students to ways that ensure adequate opportunities for literacy instruction. They can ascertain that opportunities for learning to read and write are indeed meaningful and effective *despite* the hardship students bring with them.

READING UPSIDE DOWN

There is wisdom in referencing one's own cultural and linguistic point of view when discussing *other people* and *other people's children* like Jenna. I am White. I listen, speak, read, and write in English. I grew up in a university town, went to a school district known for having pride in its diversity, and my family always had food on the table and beds to sleep in. I was also born profoundly deaf in both ears. Just 2 years before my birth, Ruby Bridges, a Black kindergartner, was one of the first to attend a court-ordered integrated school system in New Orleans. The opportunity to learn her ABCs necessitated federal marshals to escort Ruby to school for her safety. She also became a class of one as White parents removed their children from the school. In 1969, well before the passage of the Education for All Handicapped Children Act, I was quietly enrolled at my school as one of the first student in the district with a disability to be fully mainstreamed into a regular public school classroom. My parents, principal, and teachers embarked on a courageous journey to instill a rich core of language and literacy in my life at a time when many states had laws excluding students who were deaf, blind, emotionally disturbed, developmentally disabled, or otherwise considered *uneducable*.

Despite being deaf, I became a fluent reader and effective writer, and not only that, a teacher of literacy for young students. Coming full circle, I ended up as a teacher consultant for the same school district in which I grew up. However, the current climate of schools nationwide, and in my district, is vastly different from how it was when I was a child. The practice of *full inclusion*, an approach in which students with a disability spend all their time in general education, was not conceived back then but was indeed the experience I had. In fact, many federal and state programs such as special education, Title I services, English as Second Language (ESL) classes, and other educational support programs, were first initiated in the mid-1960s and 1970s in effort to "include" students from all walks of life or ability in schools. Laws to protect my rights as a person with a disability were not enacted until I was well into junior high school.

I grew up surrounded by adults at my school who had absolutely no doubt that I *could*, and *would*, learn to read and write despite not being able to hear. Although I received speech therapy from the local university, I never had to take standardized tests to monitor my literacy development during my elementary or secondary school years. I learned alongside my peers. There was no portion of my day where I was removed for "extra help" at my neighborhood school, even as I continued to catch up with my peers with my language and literacy development. It simply wasn't available in the schools then. Because I was "somehow" educated and am now fully literate, there is a widespread perception that I must have been an extremely precocious child. This is not entirely true.

I was *lucky*.

Lucky in that our progressive school principal, right in my own neighborhood, welcomed me into his school community. Lucky in that through his leadership, if there were any resistance or doubtfulness among his cadre of teachers throughout my elementary school years, I never felt it. And lucky in that my inclusive school experience occurred squarely between the final years of overt segregation and before the years of covert segregation. If I were a student earlier, I could have been placed in an institution with very little hope for my education. If I were a student today, I likely would have been tested three or more times a year, seen as an underachiever, and placed in a special education resource room for a large portion of my school days with little opportunity to strengthen my language and literacy alongside my nondisabled peers.

Because I am well aware of my luck and educational opportunities and yet still work with the constraints of the current systemic structure in our schools—one that also includes standardized testing, sorting, and tracking—the majority of my work provides support to students who are seen as having difficulty learning to read. If I must pull students out of their classrooms for short-term, focused, and individualized literacy instruction, I make sure that my students have authentic and meaningful reading and writing experiences. I avoid the use of commercial reading programs and advocate for students to have full access to the literacy curriculum in their general education classrooms. And I always work from a positive, strength-based viewpoint that *all* students are in different places of exploration of our diverse languages and literacies and that *all* students *can* achieve growth in learning to read and write in English.

Now, when I work with young students at a low horseshoe-shaped table, I sit on the floor in front of them so that I can lip-read at their height. When "listening" to students read, I read along upside down. Jenna noticed and, turning her book around to face me, she remarked that I might as well read right side up because it was all upside down to her anyway. What a twist! Despite being deaf, I was assured an opportunity to learn to read and write as a young child. Jenna, who had perfectly normal hearing, encountered roadblocks that kept her from learning to read and write. I was reading upside down because I could read. Jenna was reading upside down because she couldn't read. This book is about exploring the diversity in our languages and literacies as we all strive to help students move from *reading upside down* to *right side up*.

SHIFTING THE FOCUS FROM
ACHIEVEMENT GAPS TO OPPORTUNITY GAPS

A high level of skill and fluency in reading and writing usually leads to successful academic and economic opportunities. However, some students, like Jenna, end up feeling as if they are *reading upside down*, in that they are unable to make much sense of the letters, words, sentences, and passages they come across. This happens through no fault of their own; it is most often a result of devastating *opportunity gaps* that they have faced early in their elementary years because of subtle political, systemic, and discriminatory barriers in schools. These gaps, unfortunately, stay with students throughout their entire educational career, at times leading to unwarranted placement in special education, discipline issues, or even dropping out altogether.

There is a contentious discussion among educational researchers, educational policymakers, politicians, community members, and news media about how to resolve the issue of the achievement gap, disproportionality, and the discipline gap in schools. Indeed, for over 50 years, there has been much effort to ensure equal education for all students, regardless of race, ethnicity, national origin, religion, gender, and even disability. Despite many well-intentioned approaches, many students *still* do not have adequate opportunities to learn to read and write. By shifting the focus from an achievement gap (outcome) to an opportunity gap (cause), we begin to see that gaps in opportunities are a precursor to gaps in achievement.

Issues surrounding opportunity and achievement gaps are usually discussed on a large scale, such as the infrastructure of urban versus suburban schools. Schools in affluent suburban areas may have more competitive teacher salaries; more access to resources such as technology, updated books, and classroom material; and more class offerings and extracurricular activities (Lippman, Burns, & McArthur, 1996). However, this book is about identifying opportunity gaps on a much smaller, but certainly valuable, scale: how individual students are successfully taught to read and write. Furthermore, gaps are not limited to urban or high-poverty areas. Achievement gaps have been well documented even in diverse suburbs or small cities characterized as having high educational achievement, connections to major research universities, and ample resources (Minority Student Achievement Network, 2014).

This book is also about how opportunity gaps manifest on a local and personal level. Although different kinds of policies and programs can be implemented and even made mandatory by legal means, the bottom line is that the belief systems of the adults immediately surrounding the students—adults who have direct contact with students as classroom teachers, special education teachers, principals, mentors, and parents throughout the students' *entire* school career—have a tremendous impact. No one goes into the field of teaching without the utmost concern for the development and education of students, but teachers, particularly elementary teachers, bear the most responsibility for the challenging task of teaching students to read and write in a proficient manner. These teachers are pulled in a number of directions: curriculum standards, mandated programs, educational policy, administrators, parents, and even the students themselves. However, if the inner voices among educators define students' capabilities, opportunity gaps can occur in subtle and counterintuitive ways. To borrow the words of Glenn E. Singleton and Curtis W. Linton from their book about race in schools (2006), a "courageous conversation" is necessary. Facing our systemic shortcoming and being willing to have conversations about the true instructional needs of individual students in our schools, particularly when it comes to reading and writing, takes *courage*. We must ask ourselves: Are we, as teachers, administrators, and other educators and therapists, working as a team, *truly* teaching students to read and write? And how do we *know* that we are?

Though this book primarily focuses on opportunity gaps among students, it also demonstrates that *teachers* face opportunity gaps in their quest to *teach*. Quickly deeming teachers to be ineffective based on test scores or other educational outcomes is unproductive in ensuring high-quality education for all students. After all, it is the teachers and principals, not politicians, news reporters, or community members, who have the closest point of contact with students and their families. Because teachers are best positioned to impact students' literacy development, asking what they need in order to provide high-quality reading instruction is not only professionally empowering but also places the real responsibility on the educators in our schools.

READING RIGHT SIDE UP

Each chapter of this book describes a situation in which a student was failed by the current education system, illustrating how achievement gaps in literacy manifest themselves as missed opportunities for struggling students to learn to read and write. H. Richard Milner (2010) suggests moving away from a focus on the achievement gap to the opportunity gap. He stated:

> A focus on an achievement gap places too much blame and emphasis on students themselves as individuals and not enough attention on why gaps and disparities are commonplace in schools across the country. Opportunity, on the other hand, forces us to think about how systems, process, and institutions are overtly and covertly designed to maintain the status quo and sustain depressingly complicated disparities in education. (p. 8)

The underpinning of any reform effort contains a belief that *all* students can succeed as fluent readers. *Belief* is indeed the key word. General education teachers, in particular, play a pivotal role in providing an inclusive environment for *all* students to develop language and literacy. They are also the central point of contact and leadership in coordinating and collaborating with administrators, special education or reading intervention teachers, and other support personnel to make sure that literacy instruction in their classrooms is purposeful and meaningful to students.

Each chapter contains several stories about elementary students struggling to learn to read. Their names and other identifying information have been altered to protect their privacy. However, their situations are representative of problems that are pervasive in our schools; many students like them lag far behind in their literacy skills for a variety of reasons. Unfortunately, many of these students are labeled based on perceived deficits: They are declared "unready," have a "learning disability" or "dyslexia," are "struggling" or "impoverished," and so forth. And unfortunately, many of these students were identified by categories so often used in schools, in that they are "Title I," "special education," or "reading intervention" students. Furthermore, discussion surrounding achievement gaps involves defining racial and ethnic population groups as "Black," "African American," "Hispanic," "Latino/a," or "American Indian/Alaska Native." Making definitions, in disabling, racial, and ethnic terms, is problematic in numerous ways, which will be explored in this book. However, for the purpose of discussing opportunity gaps in schools, I refer to students' situations, ethnicity, or traits only as they seem relevant to the educational opportunities (or lack thereof) the students were afforded by the educational system. For example, I avoid the use of the negative term *minorities*, referring instead to students as having Black or Brown skin. As much as I do not like using labels or categories, for the sake of clarity, I am forced to use these terms for clarity in discussing issues related to opportunity gaps in schools. I will, however, use argue that these labels have an insidious and inadvertent tendency to create opportunity gaps because they focus on students' limits as opposed to their potential. I also believe that categories of placement or services for students, such as special education, reading intervention, Title I services, software or online programs, and even the use of teacher assistants and volunteer mentors, all function similarly in pulling students out of classrooms or aside to provide extra help in literacy. As I'll argue, this "help" is not always the best or most helpful intervention for a particular learner, and may pull students away from general instruction that could benefit them. In the end, it doesn't really matter how one names the placement or service. What matters is whether the pros of pulling students out of their regular classrooms for the "opportunity" to learn outweigh the cons, and if their "opportunity" has a meaningful influence on developing and strengthening literacy skills.

Each chapter demonstrates the crucial role of general education teachers. Most people would consider special education and other services a positive opportunity for struggling readers and do not realize the subtler opportunity gaps such programs often create for students. Even the most experienced teachers—who are guided by traditional and current teaching methods, available instructional programs, administrative rules, and even their colleagues and mentor teachers—most likely see special education (or other services that provide extra help) as a positive opportunity. However, as the stories in this book illustrate, the help these students tend to get is not always helpful when it comes to learning to read. Although they may be distressing for both general and special educators to hear, these stories depict opportunity gaps in truly unexpected ways—unexpected in that the teachers and administrators involved thought they were doing what was best for the students. Therefore, the purpose of this book is not to minimize the importance of special education, Title I, ESL, and reading intervention teachers but to redefine their position as supportive to instruction by general education teachers, rather than as a substitute for general education instruction. Accordingly, each chapter imagines a way in which a classroom teacher might proactively change the trajectory of the student(s) profiled.

Each chapter is also an attempt to bring responsibility, professional judgment, and decisionmaking back to educators where it belongs, rather than allowing it to be subject to the whims and beliefs of policymakers, most of whom have never stood up in front of a classroom full of eager,

rambunctious young students, let alone dealt with the struggles and challenges elementary school teachers face on a daily basis. Each chapter closes
with a series of questions educators can use to guide them in making decisions on behalf of the students—even within the limits of mandated policies—that honor and appreciate students' exploration of literacy while also
giving them the educational opportunities they require.

And each chapter also brings a call for change and hope . . . hope so
that most *all* students can move from *reading upside down* to *reading right
side up*, and hope that once they are reading right side up, they will be better
prepared for success in colleges and careers across our country.

CHAPTER 1

'Tis the Good Reader
That Makes the Good Book

As a 1st-grader, Bree noted to her mom with great revelation that even after her class had celebrated 100 days of school, it still seemed that half of the kids in her class had not yet learned to read. Trevin was one of these students. Learning the alphabet, handling books and turning their pages, and acquiring pleasure and knowledge from stories was a whole new world for him when he started school. In fact, when Trevin pretended to read a book during independent reading time and individual reading lessons, he held it up like a teacher reading to the whole class. Because Trevin had never had a book placed in front of him on his lap, nor had he seen his mother read, it took him time to realize books are meant to be read independently, with the book facing him.

THE VIEW OF STUDENTS AS "UNREADY" OR "AT-RISK"

Trevin was considered an "unready" or "at-risk" student the moment he was enrolled in 1st grade. His teacher was concerned enough about Trevin to make a formal request for a referral to special education after 2 months of school. Most students, like Bree, who enter school in kindergarten or 1st grade, come with a range of experiences with books and other sources of print, such as newspapers, letters, emails, and grocery lists. Although some students are already readers, others have never been read aloud to in their young lives. Interactions with literacy for many students begin as early as 2 or 3 years old, but for some, opportunities for literacy interaction don't begin until they start formal schooling.

Not only do students bring a significant range of literacy experiences in kindergarten or 1st grade, but teachers in later grades also confront a wide range of reading abilities, having students who read up to several grade levels below expectations. Their concern for these students was heightened by the hopeful national goal that "by the year 2000, all children in America will start school ready to learn" (National Education Goals Panel, 1990). Too often, concerned teachers quickly refer Trevin and other students viewed as "unready" or "at-risk" upon entering school or subsequent grade levels to a team of support professionals, such as reading intervention, Title I, English as Second Language (ESL), family or adult literacy, and special education educators. Remedial programs are not always effective, particularly in special education. "This segment of the population has been unlucky—in some cases tragically so. Some special education students are born with severe limitations that affect their ability to learn. Others are not so much disabled at birth as they are ill-served by an education system that generally fails to respond well to individual needs and circumstances" (Finn & Petrilli, 2012, p. 2). Although it appeared to his teacher that Trevin needed an evaluation for special educa-tion, he simply didn't have the typical level of interaction with literacy prior to 1st grade that our educational system requires of students. This lack of exposure by no means equates to a developmental delay or learning disability. Furthermore, a study (Sullivan & Field, 2013) investigating preschoolers with mild to moderate delays who received preschool special education found that on average they had lower scores in reading and math in kindergarten than similar students who did not receive such services. When students viewed as "unready" or "at-risk" are removed from classrooms for intervention, they work on fragmented and isolated skills in an environment that lacks rich lan-guage and literacy. Jenna, the student portrayed in the Preface, was consid-ered a "late bloomer," placed in special education, and was still not reading past a kindergarten level by 4th grade. Though Trevin's teacher had good intentions in requesting a formal referral for special education, Trevin's expe-rience is likely to mirror Jenna's. In other words, the help that students con-sidered "unready" or "at-risk" receive in remedial programs may not be the kind of help they need or that they will benefit from. Both Jenna and Trevin would have far richer experiences in exploring and interacting with language and literacy in fully inclusive classrooms.

PROBLEMS WITH TRADITIONAL CONSTRUCTS OF SCHOOL READINESS

Although there is no consistent definition for readiness, psychometrics usu-ally present readiness as some combination of cognitive, psychomotor, and social-emotional development that is congruent with children's chronological age. "Different theories of readiness depict a variety of mechanisms for readiness development, but all seem to agree that readiness is something *within* the child that is necessary for success in school" (Graue, 1993, p. 4). Measures of readiness compare skills among children who later have successful school experiences, primarily in terms of achievement in literacy, with those who are not considered to have had a successful experience. The traditional construct of readiness has been based on assumptions that there is a predetermined set of capabilities that all children need before they enter school (National Association for the Education of Young Children, 1995). Trevin was caught in this quandary, a situation beyond his control.

Readiness includes emergent literacy or beginning reading skills, such as concepts of print, book-handling abilities, letter recognition, phonemic awareness, and sight word knowledge, and is linked to positive outcomes in reading and writing achievement. Trevin was already "failing" to meet literacy expectations right at the start of his school career without ever having had an opportunity to be exposed to literacy. Studies on early reading skills invariably end up acknowledging correlates among population groups such as by gender, race/ethnicity, poverty status, parents' highest level of education, family type, and primary home language (Mulligan, Hastedt, & Carlivati McCarroll, 2012). Not all children enter school equally prepared to learn to read, and those from the nation's most economically disadvantaged families are least likely to be well prepared to succeed (National Early Literacy Panel, 2009). The problem with the traditional construct of reading readiness is that the curriculum begins with an assumption that students already have concepts of print, book-handling abilities, letter recognition, phonemic awareness, and sight word knowledge in English at the start of kindergarten or 1st grade. When the curriculum builds on this assumption, Trevin and other students who have not had these literacy experiences are immediately left behind.

In attempts to determine causes of achievement gaps besides reading readiness, studies have pointed to many correlates such as poverty, poor nutrition, low birth weight, exposure to heavy metals, amount of television watching, single parenting, and parental involvement. From the research and statistics now available, Barton and Coley (2009) determined that it remains clear that minority and poor students continue to face conditions that undermine school achievement. They went on to say that "the achievement gap has deep roots—deep in out-of-school experiences and deep in the structures of schools" (p. 33). Trevin exhibited some of these risk factors, living in poverty with a single parent. However, schools have little control over out-of-school experiences other than to objectively acknowledge them and to try to minimize the risk factors within the structures of school in order to avoid perpetuating cycles of risks from generation to generation. Furthermore, having risk factors does not automatically mean that there is a cognitive incapacity for learning at school. Even though Trevin was living in poverty with a single parent, he was still using language and learning about the world around him, a world that happens to be different, not disabling, from the mainstream culture that schools maintain.

Research has shown striking disparity in the language development of children from different socioeconomic levels. Because language and literacy are interrelated and because Trevin was not read aloud to as a preschooler, his teacher suspected that his language development was lagging behind that of students like Bree. In studying educational differences stemming from the variation in everyday experiences of young American children, Hart and Risley (2003) noted a 30-million-word gap between children from a professional family and children from a welfare family. Their data provided the first approximation of the significance of children's early language experiences, suggesting the huge scope of the intervention task needed to provide equal experiences and thus equal opportunities to children living in poverty. Another study found significant disparities in language proficiency in relation to family socioeconomic status was already evident at 18 months of age, and that by 24 months, there was a 6-month gap between higher- and lower-SES families (Fernald, Marchman, & Weisleder, 2013). Differences in socioeconomic status are associated with variation in language growth and, in turn, are considered predictive of later academic success. However, schools making distinctions between lack of opportunities for rich interaction with language and literacy versus actual reading difficulties are able to provide appropriate instruction or intervention for individual students. Language gap aside, Trevin was at a different point from Bree in his discovery of literacy, and his language would only develop further with more authentic literature throughout his entire school days.

Because traditional constructs of school readiness require children to develop certain capabilities before they begin formal schooling, the impacts of parents' educational attainment and parental literacy on young children's literacy learning has been widely studied. Supported by research in emergent literacy (Strickland & Morrow, 1989; Sulzby, 1985), family literacy initiatives proliferated as a means to support literacy development in children outside of school (Morrow, Paratore, Gaber, Harrison, & Tracey, 1993; Nickse, 1989). Most scholars agree that parents are children's first teachers and that reading and writing begins at home (Clay, 1979, 1987), so the school suspected Trevin's mother was a factor in his unfamiliarity with books. However, helplessly viewing parents as being incapable or irresponsible providers of literacy or homework help without ensuring that students have opportunities for authentic interaction with literacy at school is unproductive for students like Trevin.

Despite valuable research into foundational ways children begin to understand concepts of literacy long before they begin to read and write conventionally, ethnographic research has also shown that home literacy practices do not always map clearly onto specific "school-like" literacy tasks. Family literacy programs that focus on teaching parents to do "school-like" activities in the home assume that parents lack the skills essential to promoting school success and are not based on sound research (Auerbach, 1989). In debunking myths and stereotypes creating images of poor, inner-city families as illiterate or unread, Taylor and Dorsey-Gaines (1988) stated that one's level of education (such as completing high school) and literacy cannot be used interchangeably in research and policy. A review of existing ideas and programs also suggests that families are too often viewed through their deficits and dilemmas rather than the richness of their heritages and experiences (Morrow, Paratore, Gaber, Harrison, & Tracey, 1993). Trevin, being already viewed as having a "deficit" in literacy, it also seemed to the schools that Trevin's mother had "deficits" in her ability to raise him. However, his mother felt that her role was to raise a child and that his school's role was to raise a reader. Programs aimed at increasing school readiness and closing achievement gaps need to be mindful of the cultural context in which children are raised, being sure to focus on culturally relevant practices as beneficial for children's development (Dotterer, Iruka, & Pungello, 2012). Disconnect in partnerships between home and school occur when teachers and administrators assume that parents lack the ability or willingness to promote "school-like" success in their children, creating the pervasive but often false sense that these parents do not care about their children's education.

Preschool and prekindergarten programs are increasingly viewed by educators and policymakers as an intervention for children living in poverty, such as Head Start, or for children with disabilities under an amendment to Education for All Handicapped Children Act. Evaluating students' school readiness involves assessing "deficits;" it determines things that children do not know, such as a certain number of letters of the alphabet. "This sort of assessment is looking backwards and is actually more an assessment of the learning environments of children prior to school entry than of the learning capabilities of the children themselves" (Farran, 2011, p. 6). With this viewpoint, it is easy to lament that Trevin hadn't received early childhood intervention to address issues with "readiness" for school. Many teachers feel helpless when they are unable to take the initiative to provide literacy interaction from whatever starting point their students are.

Alternatively, many children are enrolled in accredited preschool programs with a professional staff of certified early childhood teachers, some with tuitions rivaling college costs. Though "from 1980 to 2011, the percentage of 3- to 5-year-olds enrolled in preprimary programs increased from 53 percent to 64 percent" (Aud, Wilkinson-Flicker, Kristapovich, Rathbun, Wang, & Zhang, 2013, p. 44), not all families have the means, or the value for cultural or personal reasons, to access such programs. Because children coming from families with risk factors are likely to attend schools in high-poverty neighborhoods struggling to promote high achievement, Farran (2011) pointed out that it is very difficult to disentangle the effects of school readiness from the effects of the elementary or primary grade schools students attend. Therefore, Farran urged educators to rethink concepts of school readiness as well as place more careful thought about school experiences itself. Trevin came to school without early literacy experiences, so the quality of early years *at school* is paramount for his success in his educational career.

Well-meaning intentions, initiatives, and funding to establish programs for addressing reading readiness; socioeconomic conditions; and gaps in language development, family literacy, and access to preschool are based on a long history of deficit thinking. Deficit approaches uphold mindsets in which responsibility is placed on students and their families to fit into the dominant language and culture *before* they have equal access to an education. Valencia (1997) remarked that a framework of deficit thinking is a person-centered explanation of school failure, particularly among individuals who have cultural, linguistic, and economic differences, while "institutional structures and inequitable schooling arrangements that exclude students from learning are held exculpatory" (p. 9).

DISTINGUISHING ACHIEVEMENT GAPS VERSUS OPPORTUNITY GAPS

Neither Bree nor Trevin had control over the home literacy environments in which they started their young lives. Bree was *lucky* and Trevin *unlucky* to match up with so-called grade level expectations by the time they entered 1st grade. As a result, Trevin was at risk for being underserved by an education system that fails to respond to his starting point as a capable learner of language and literacies. Exclusion can start very early in life (United Nations Educational, Scientific and Cultural Organization, 2009). It is not a question of incapability or lack of achievement on Trevin's part. Rather, he had little opportunity to learn in an "academic manner" before starting school.

The Achievement Gap	The Opportunity Gap
Achievement gaps can occur when young students like Trevin, who lack school-like literacy experiences prior to entering kindergarten or 1st grade and whose underlying concepts of how books work and why we read has not yet been fostered, are seen as making unsatisfactory growth in reading instruction early on in their school career.	Trevin's gap is not necessarily a result of a lack of literacy exposure itself but rather a lack of access to a high-quality reading curriculum and instruction beginning with what the students know (or do not know) and building upon that knowledge.

Achievement gaps carry a mindset in which the burden of meeting educational benchmarks is placed on individual students before they even have access to education. Recognizing opportunity gaps, on the other hand, shifts the culpability for inequality to the institutional barriers and standards that make equal access to an education out of reach for some students.

Opportunity gaps occur when educators and policymakers define literacy and readiness. The reality is that American schools—mandated, designed, and staffed by educators who overwhelmingly represent dominant language and culture—are the very determinants and gatekeepers of literacy learning. This system therefore enables only students who possess a language and culture similar to their educators' to succeed with ease. Lazar, Edwards, and McMillon (2012) encourage educators to explore the "interrelationship between literacy, language, culture, identity, and power, and its importance when it comes to seeing students' literacy potential, building on their existing knowledge, and helping them access school-valued literacies and languages" (p. 47). A gap in opportunities to learn is a precursor to gaps in achievement.

The definition of literacy is complex and controversial. The term implies an interaction between social demands and individual competence (Venezky, 1995). The United Nations Educational, Scientific and Cultural Organization (UNESCO; 2004) defines *literacy* as the "ability to identify, understand, interpret, create, communicate and compute, using printed and written materials associated with varying contexts" (p. 13). Attempts to define literacy have led to the use of various categories such as academic literacy, media literacy, cultural literacy, workplace literacy, and computer literacy and can be seen as a continuum with terms such as illiteracy and functional literacy.

Priorities for literacy learning are both personal and cultural. Some families want their children to be informed citizens of our society and to be able to read newspapers and books discussing different perspectives and values. Others want their children to be able to read their religious scriptures or be well read in the classics. Some families are literate in their native language but not in English. Some families place emphasis on oral storytelling over print. Some may feel reading is of little necessity to them, taking a viewpoint that those who need to consult a manual in order to repair a car must be, in a sense, quite unintelligent. Trevin's mother wanted Trevin to learn to read and write for success in school. Ferdman (1990) explains that "an illiterate person is someone who cannot access (or produce) texts that are seen as significant within a given culture. That same person, in another cultural context, may be classified as being quite literate. When a number of cultures coexist within the same society, it is more likely that we will encounter variant concepts of what constitutes being literate" (p. 186). In a culturally and linguistically heterogeneous society where compulsory education exists, variant concepts of what constitutes being literate are sure to conflict. However, there is no need for conflict. There is no form of literacy that is "right" or "legitimate." "Instead of discussing 'literacy,' a more accurate and inclusive way to describe practices that surround language and print is to say 'literacies'" (Lazar, Edwards, & McMillon, 2012, p. 47). When we embrace and empower this viewpoint, opportunities abound for learning and strengthening language, culture, identity, and literacies for all students.

As difficult it is to agree on a sole definition of literacy, reaching an agreement on defining readiness and at-risk characteristics is equally problematic. Any definition of school readiness places the burden on individual students, like Trevin, to somehow fit into a preconceived set of benchmarks in order to access an education that is authentic and inclusive. Despite differing definitions of literacy and readiness, most families want their children to succeed in school and, later, in places of employment. Although many families take on a large role in teaching their children to read and write, others expect schools to do the teaching. Therefore, if teachers view "their students' literacy and language abilities as substandard, they may not design their instruction in a way that targets their students' actual potential" (Lazar, Edwards, & McMillon, 2012, p. 46). Instead, schools can respect families in the cultivation of their own literacies and the level of parent–school involvment they are comfortable with, and still take the sole responsibility for teaching chldren to read in an authentic and purposeful manner.

CHANGING THE TRAJECTORY OF STUDENTS
VIEWED AS "UNREADY" OR "AT-RISK"

Trevin, first viewed as an "unready" or "at-risk" student, was referred for special education within 2 months of his enrollment at school. Changing Trevin's educational trajectory could have started with a teacher who viewed him as eager to learn and capable of learning. Trevin was indeed learning school-like literacy by copying his teacher's literate behavior when she held books up for all to see. A teacher operating from this positive viewpoint would have appreciated Trevin's current literacy level and recognized opportunities to help his literacy grow, teaching him ways of handling books, making connections from speech to print, and conceptualizing what reading is all about.

To help Trevin and students like him develop academic literacy, classroom teachers can build upon students' strengths, provide developmentally appropriate and culturally sensitive instruction, and ensure access to and provide authentic experiences with books and other sources of print. In an inclusive classroom that recognizes his developing literacy, Trevin can continue to listen to stories read aloud by his teacher. He can participate in the discussions following the stories. He can crawl into the lap of an adult for a "bedtime story." He can join a guided reading group, receive individual reading lessons, and do shared reading with Bree and his peers. He can read from a collection of memorized books or listen to books digitally during independent reading time. Trevin can communicate and share his writing, even if it's drawing or scribbling or uses invented spellings. Trevin can interact with sources of print during play such as cookbooks in the housekeeping corner, architectural specifications in the building blocks areas, or timetables in the transportation unit.

There is no need take a pathological stance that Trevin is "unready" or "at-risk" or to remove him from his classroom or provide him a prescription for a specialized or separate reading program. Ensuring that Trevin is surrounded with close attention and scaffolding in an authentic environment rich with language and literacy along with his peers makes it clear to him, his parents, his peers, and other adults in the school that he belongs there and that he is going to learn alongside his peers. In this kind of inclusive environment, Bree is also able to continue her educational path and be part of a classroom that has "the most effective means of combating discriminatory attitudes, creating welcoming communities, building an inclusive society, and achieving education for all" (United Nations Educational, Scientific, and Cultural Organization, 1994, p. ix). Both Trevin and Bree can learn to see that there are many forms of language and literacies in our global society.

Taking on the View of Ready Students

*Does your inner voice use the terms unready or at-risk to
categorize students? Listen to it carefully. How can you ensure
that your thinking about students is proactive and positive?*

"The only legally and ethically defensible criterion for determining school
entry is whether the child has reached the legal chronological age of school
entry. While arbitrary, this criterion is also fair" (National Association for
the Education of Young Children, 1995, p. 2). By redefining the concept of
"readiness" and asserting that all students *are* ready, teachers can create an
environment in which *both* Trevin and Bree can grow, one that supports
exploration and development of language and literacy on a full day-to-day
basis. By rejecting any notion of redshirting kindergartners, retention, or
covert segregation at any grade, teachers can make it clear to their colleagues, administrators, parents, and stakeholders that they are accepting
all students as rightful members of their classrooms.

All Kinds of Families and All Kinds of Literacies

*Some families provide an environment rich in literacy and others
feel it is the school's job to teach their children to read and
write when they get to kindergarten or 1st grade. How can you
acknowledge the multiple forms of literacies students and their
families bring to school and accept responsibility for teaching
students who have a wide range of experience with academic
literacy? In what ways can you start with and build upon what
students already know about language and literacies?*

By demonstrating full inclusion for students of culturally, linguistically, and
academically diverse backgrounds, teachers are well positioned to support
students' exploration, bridge their languages and literacies, and ensure
their continuing growth in reading and writing in more standardized forms
of English. "Families can, of course, learn a great deal about literacy development from the school, but it is also true that teachers need to learn
more about how parents and children share literacy on a daily basis and
to explore how such events can serve school learning" (Morrow, Paratore,
Gaber, Harrison, & Tracey, 1993, p. 197). Teachers can make an effort
to get to know families, develop rapport, and build trust. They can avoid
relying on parents to read aloud to children or request help with teaching
at home. Opportunities for literacy interaction and classroom support for

students should be provided at school instead of suggesting costly tutoring. Resources for economic and social support should be offered when sought by the families, but not judgmentally "prescribed" by schools.

Developing a Flexible and Responsive Curriculum

How can you structure your classroom environment and curriculum routines so all students are included and engaged in literacy activities?

Teachers can develop exploration centers, open-ended assignments, and flexible guided reading and writing groups so *all* students have access to a wide array of materials for learning to their fullest capabilities. "Rather than imposing rigid, lock-step distinctions between grades, schools must be able to offer continuous progress for children through the primary grades, recognizing that children's developmental timetables do not conform to the yearly calendar" (National Association for the Education of Young Children, 1995, p. 3). Even the Common Core State Standards (2012) recognize that "no set of grade-specific standards can fully reflect the great variety in abilities, needs, learning rates, and achievement levels of students in any given classroom." Teachers have the flexibility to expand their literacy instruction for all students—including those like both Trevin and Bree—instead of adhering to narrowly prescribed and grade-specific texts and worksheets.

Taking Back Ownership and Leadership

How are you taking ownership—and leadership—in mobilizing support staff such as reading intervention teachers, reading coaches, in-class parent and community volunteers, and guest readers without passing students viewed as "unready" or "at-risk" off to someone else?

Too often, students considered unready or at-risk in reading become the responsibility of someone other than the general education teacher. Failure to maintain an on-schedule pace of reading acquisition is the most frequent basis for referral to an instructional support program such as remedial or special education (Walmsley & Allington, 1995). When teachers make referrals, they usually have underlying systemic backing from educational administrators monitoring assessment scores, political mandates in curriculum design, and assessments from core reading programs. Therefore, teachers and administrators usually see referrals as opportunities for students to "catch up." However, when educators look for a remedial approach outside of the classroom in order to meet a student's instructional needs, they are still retaining a deficit viewpoint, especially when linguistic and cultural differences are viewed from a socially stratified standpoint. As a result of this kind of thinking, students who enter remedial or special education almost never have true opportunities to catch up. Teachers should seek the support of reading intervention teachers and special educators to improve their teaching or provide accommodations inside the classroom while still taking ownership and leadership for the day-to-day instructional decisions about a student's growth in reading and writing. If the responsibility for the individual needs of students is passed to someone other than the general education teacher, the stage is being set for exclusionary practices in the student's educational narrative.

Maximizing the Effectiveness of Community Volunteers

> *How are you creating a welcoming environment in which parents and community members can help support students' language and literacies?*

Inviting parents and community members into classrooms and schools can make valuable contributions to developing an environment that supports language and literacies. However, it is not enough simply to invite them; it is important to make sure that they feel welcome in the school setting. And it is also important that those who read to students (or listen to students read) during class time know how they can be open to diversity discussions surrounding books. Some parents and community members may recall negative educational experiences from their own childhoods. Some may perceive assumptions and judgment about their abilities to contribute to a traditional school setting based on media reports that identify parents as part of the problematic nationwide achievement gap. Still others would prefer to leave the teaching to the "professionals." By cherishing families from linguistically and culturally diverse backgrounds, warm and welcoming educators create an environment in which all are not just invited but *encouraged* to be part of the village raising our children and making positive contributions to achievement and literacy rates.

Rethinking Book Fairs and Pajama Nights

> *Literacy events such as book fairs and pajama nights are often inaccessible for families in high-poverty or culturally nondominant communities and families who may lack extra*

cash, time, or transportation. Thus, these events perpetuate a sense of privilege in which only like-minded families can participate, marginalizing others. How can you advocate for and ensure equity in such events without coming across as charitable?

Extracurricular literacy events are planned with the best intention of bridging home–school partnerships and promoting reading for pleasure at home. However, the educators who plan these events need to consider them carefully from the perspectives of the diverse families they invite. Some families will not accept "book tokens" or "prizes," feeling they are a form of charity. Some families have parents who work two jobs to make ends meet, or they may work the night shift, making it impossible to reconcile attendance at such events with their work schedule. Some may not have the means for transportation or do not want to risk public transportation after dark. Some families may have other children to care for. Encouraging diverse parent organizations and committees that match the overall demographics of the school in which all members contribute ideas will help craft literacy events that meet the needs of a diverse body of students and their families.

CLOSING THE BEGINNING OPPORTUNITY GAP FOR ALL STUDENTS

As established in this chapter, taking on a view of "unreadiness" and "risk" is unproductive to both students and the community at large. When educators and policymakers define literacy and readiness for learning to read and write, it is a political determination that has a big linguistic, cultural, and economic impact on students and their families. Furthermore, a system that relies on measuring students against age-related benchmarks allows schools to hold on to a deficit model of education, which in turn creates exclusionary practices and achievement gaps very early on in a student's educational career. Teachers who have intimate day-to-day teaching interactions with students are in the position to change students' trajectory as capable learners. Educators, policymakers, curriculum designers, and parents can be encouraged take the positive viewpoint that *all* students are ready for school and each subsequent grade. With an increasingly diverse population, we can no longer maintain a traditional educational environment in which only a select few can succeed.

CHAPTER 2

Checking the Weather

Elise, a 2nd-grader, was a slow, letter-by-letter reader. She read *cat* as *c-a-t* and *dog* as *d-o-g*. She attempted to sound out irregular words letter-by-letter— for example, reading *some* as *so-me* and *my* as *m-why*, pronouncing these words literally. Because she focused heavily on phonics, Elise had little reading comprehension. She was negative about her capabilities when it came to reading, often saying she was bad at it. She even used escape tactics to avoid reading, such as hiding in bathrooms, offering to run errands to the office and taking her time returning, making frequent trips to sharpen her pencils, and otherwise clowning around.

By contrast, Natalie utilized her vast background knowledge when asked to read instead of decoding. She got the gist of things well enough that she could guess her way along in school. Because Natalie was well behaved, verbally articulate, and wasn't easily spotted as a student with potential difficulties, she bided her time through 2nd and 3rd grade. By 4th grade, her reading comprehension sank, and it sank deeply. Although she could read basic consonant-vowel-consonant (short) words and had a repertoire of sight words, she found multisyllabic (long) words difficult to deal with, including root words with prefixes and suffixes, and by 4th grade, there were no longer illustrations to support her reading. In her 4th-grade classroom, Natalie had a teacher who focused on her lack of reading skills and was at all not swayed by her sweet personality. Natalie started to have vague symptoms of stomachaches and fatigue, and she no longer wanted to come to school, much to the chagrin of her worried parents.

Joshua was a shy 3rd-grade child who was a highly accurate reader. He could use decoding strategies to tackle unknown words. He knew many sight words automatically. Although his fluency was clocked at an average speed (as indicated by a grade-level assessment), his expression was always flat and he had difficulty comprehending what he had read. It was arduous

14

for Joshua to retell a story or passage. He couldn't connect what he read with his own knowledge and experiences. He would squirm around in his seat and scratch his head while looking at the text. When asked to summarize a story, his typical response would be, "Well, um, err . . . this is about . . . let me read it again." He would read it over again. The next response would be along the lines of "Well, let's see, this is about a pirate named Jake." When asked, "So what about the pirate named Jake? What happened to Jake?" he would have to read the text all over again. It became cumbersome to get high-quality responses from Joshua. It was no surprise that as he started to fall behind in the middle of 2nd grade, Joshua became reluctant to read, declaring it a "sissy" activity, and was usually found "off-task" during reading time.

Elise, Natalie, and Joshua, considered "struggling readers," were referred for evaluation as possibly having a learning disability, language impairment, childhood depression, or attention deficit disorder/attention deficit/hyperactivity disorder (ADD/ADHD). They were all viewed as having some sort of cognitive or emotional deficit within themselves but there was little thought about the quality of their instruction. The reading instruction they had received was from one-size-fits-all reading programs, and in a world with many diverse learners, the key is matching the right intervention to the strengths and weaknesses of the individual.

VIEWING READERS AS "STRUGGLING"

Elise, Natalie, and Joshua are viewed as "struggling readers." Too often, when children are found to be struggling with reading, there is immediate concern as to what might be wrong with them; it is often suggested that they may have a learning disability, language impairment, childhood depression, or even ADD/ADHD. Elementary teachers are familiar with children who read at a slow, halting pace or who are reluctant to read altogether. These are children who rarely catch up with their peers and have difficulty accessing content, including mathematics, science, social studies, and other academic subjects. Many times these children feel poorly about school as well. In keeping with a diagnostic mindset that seeks a cause *within* these children, there is a tendency for teachers and administrators to remove such children from the general education curriculum for additional instruction, which may not even be provided by professionals with expertise in differentiated reading instruction. Allington (2011) noted that in far too many schools, at-risk kindergartners and 1st-graders receive no expert additional instruction. Instead, schools spend enormous amounts of money on a variety of approaches, such as the use of paraprofessionals, computer-based instructional programs, and core reading programs, that don't work. The current system of grade retention, segregated remediation programs, special education, and harsh disciplinary policies—all placing fault within "struggling readers" themselves—remains entrenched and unproductive in many of our schools.

The reality is that Elise, Natalie, and Joshua were trying to learn to read in the way they were taught. Their schools, likely having gone through stormy external and internal debates on which instructional approaches should be implemented in their classrooms, settled on a one-size-fits-all reading program. Ultimately, a few students, like Elise, Natalie, and Joshua, need a form of instruction that is missing from the mandated reading program. In other words, they were caught without an umbrella.

THE QUEST TO FIND THE BEST READING PROGRAM

The field of teaching reading is akin to the field of meteorology. Everyone is an expert on weather. There are meteorologists with advanced degrees, newscasters who give morning and evening updates, farmers, amateur weather junkies, and, of course, grandmothers who feel it in their bones. The tools we use to study weather give mixed results. Likewise, just about everyone is an expert on how to teach reading. We have our share of specialists with advanced degrees, along with schoolteachers, reading program publishers, and private tutors. We have caring parents with their own personal experiences. And we have politicians. The tools to assess texts for their readability levels or children for their reading achievement are also imprecise. However, like attempts to forecast the weather, there is no single reading intervention or program that will work predictably for all learners. The "reading wars"— disputes over the "correct" approach to reading instruction—led educators, policymakers, parents, and community members to the belief that the key to helping students was identifying a single approach to teaching reading. When one instructional approach was mandated or implemented without reference to a particular student's individual skills or literacy background, many students suffered from the imposition of a program ill-suited to their particular situation.

The reading wars, between proponents of teaching phonics versus whole language, were waged primarily in the 1980s and 1990s. Because policymakers were using results from reading research in a selective, uneven, and opportunistic manner (Pearson, 2004), overly simplistic arguments for or against phonics or whole language were proclaimed particularly among politicians and in media headlines (Flippo, 1999). Yet, virtually every major synthesis on reading during and since the days of the "reading wars" rejected the simple dualism between phonics and whole language and instead encouraged instruction that focused on helping children master both the alphabetic principle and the acquisition of meaning from text (Kim, 2008). "The idea of a one-way-only approach, and the war that has been built around that idea, has not come from the reading community of researchers" (Flippo, 1999, p. 38) but politicians and reporters. Though it may seem that public debate in education have moved on to other educational topics, policies toward the teaching of reading, which are mandated and implemented by states, school districts, or even internal departments within districts, have not always reflected a move away from dualism. Local school board members or school administrators seek simple solutions nowadays through the purchase of commercially made and prescribed products. Still, "when they find that the current ones don't really work, they can easily switch to other philosophies, inaccurately again, still going for simplicity and 'absolutes'" (Flippo, 1999, p. 39). When students like Elise, Natalie, and Joshua are being taught as if there is only one so-called "expert" way of teaching reading, despite the differences in their reading challenges and strengths, it becomes clear that there are victims early on in the educational system—and that students like Elise, Natalie, and Joshua are among them. These students were on their way to being identified as "learning disabled" or "dyslexic" or given some other intrinsic label pertaining to a biological, cognitive, or motivational problem as within these students.

Children who learned to read "naturally" became readers by listening to stories, building a core of vocabulary words through their life experiences, learning about letters and words in their environment and in text, playing around with rhymes, and experimenting with writing. Yet there is a plethora of commercial products—complete with materials, workbooks, and even technological tools and software—that schools and parents purchase to teach or improve the skills of developing or "struggling" readers like Elise, Natalie, and Joshua. Reading programs make promotional claims that say their methods for teaching reading are grounded in research; adopting a program just because it is evidence-based, however, does not guarantee reading success (International Reading Association, 2002). One reason struggling readers receive fewer high-quality reading lessons is our fixation with one-size-fits-all core reading programs, programs that require little actual reading, do not promote high-success reading, and do not offer self-selected reading (Allington, 2011). Without teacher discretion and a watchful monitoring system to ensure that an instructional approach or reading program is effective for each individual, children will fall through the cracks.

Many children who do not achieve reading proficiency in a timely manner are identified as having a learning disability or even dyslexia. However, one of the most controversial issues in the field of learning disabilities pertains to its definition and construction. Currently, the Individuals with Disabilities Education Act (IDEA) holds a simplistic definition for Specific Learning Disabilities (SLD) as "a disorder in one or more of the basic psychological processes involved in understanding or in using language, spoken or written, that may manifest itself in the imperfect ability to listen, think, speak, read, write, spell, or to do mathematical calculations" (U.S. Department of Education, 2014). Likewise, the field of dyslexia has been "unable to produce a universally accepted definition that is not imprecise, amorphous, or difficult to operationalize" (Elliott & Grigorenko, 2014, p. 5). Currently, dyslexia is broadly defined as a "developmental reading disability, presumably congenital and perhaps heredity that may vary in degree from mild to severe" (Harris & Hodges, 1995, p. 63). Both SLD and dyslexia are also defined by ruling out other factors that may impact learning. Learning disabilities and dyslexia do not include "learning problems as resulting from visual, hearing, or motor disabilities, of mental retardation, of emotional disturbance, or of environmental, cultural, or economic disadvantage" (U.S. Department of Education, 2014). (Unfortunately, the terms mental retardation and environmental, cultural, or economic disadvantage are still referred to in the federal regulations. Even though these terms are no longer accepted in educational and research dialogue, the impact of cultural, linguistic, and economic differences among individual students can still be misperceived as a cognitive impairment, mental health issue, or learning disability.)

From the beginning of the field of learning disabilities, a characteristic feature of learning disabilities is the unexplained, and unexpected, reasons for underachievement in an academic domain. This unexpectedness has been constructed as the discrepancy between a general learning potential (represented by intelligence in the average or above-average range) on the one hand and poor scholastic achievement on the other hand (Buttner & Shamir, 2011). In other words, there is no clear manifestation of learning disabilities; learning disabilities is simply a way of describing a "condition" of underachievement for unknown reasons. Though the basic definition of learning disabilities has not changed in over 40 years and there is no agreement on its specificity, the focus has now shifted to *operational* definitions of SLD necessary for the practical purpose of identifying a student as "learning disabled" (Kavale, Spaulding, & Beam, 2009, p. 46). One operational definition of learning disabilities involved the discrepancy model in that students with "learning disabilities" have normal intelligence but are found to be reading far below their grade level. In some cases, the students had to wait long enough until a discrepancy was severe enough, usually around 3rd or 4th grade, to qualify for instructional support. This waiting period generated widespread claims among educators that the severe discrepancy model was ultimately a *wait-to-fail* model.

In an attempt to lessen the impact of the severe discrepancy model and address wait-to-fail situations, the reauthorization of IDEA in 2004 stated that "prior to, or as a part of, referral processes for identification of learning disabilities, data must demonstrate the child was provided *appropriate instruction* (emphasis added) in regular education settings" (U.S. Department of Education, 2006a). Yet, defining "appropriate instruction" is subjective, for quests to find the "best program" for teaching reading are controversial and often unsuccessful as well.

Because intelligence versus academic assessment of children is no longer the focus when it comes to identifying learning disabilities, Response-to-Intervention (RTI) models of intervention and diagnoses are being widely implemented in schools throughout our country. RTI is a process that schools can use to help children who are struggling academically or behaviorally. There is no single, absolute definition of RTI (Center for Parent Information and Resources, 2012); however, "it is commonly understood to represent a meaningful integration of assessment and intervention within a multilevel system to prevent school failure" (Fuchs & Fuchs, 2009, p. 250). The majority of states have adopted models that include three or four levels, or tiers, of intervention, with each tier offering increasingly differentiated or more intensive small-group or individualized instruction (Berkeley, Bender, Peaster, & Saunders, 2009). Thus, instead of assessing for discrepancies between students' cognitive and academic abilities, schools are now looking at achievement data, sorting students into tiers, and providing "intervention," often of a commercial nature, that may or may not ultimately meet students' individual needs. Reynolds and Shaywitz (2009) noted that many diagnoses of learning disabilities are made when achievement levels are persistently below grade-level standards and there is lack of progress relative to peers. They opined that RTI is yet another discrepancy-based model now being between the achievement of an individual student as compared with the achievement of his or her peers in the school.

Even though RTI is an attempt to provide immediate intervention, the inordinate level of guesswork in the identification of learning disabilities continues to be problematic and potentially detrimental for readers viewed as "struggling" or "at-risk." Some children who have gone through the RTI process successfully may still turn out to have a disability. Conversely, children who are found to "fail" RTI may not necessarily have a disability.

Although it is intuitively appealing to argue that RTI is a strong process for ruling out disability, RTI cannot be applied accurately, even in this manner (Reynolds & Shaywitz, 2009). Because the reading research field is fraught with controversy over best practices to begin with, "our conceptualization of what reading is and how it is acquired will greatly influence how we define dyslexia, what we think causes problems in learning to read, and what we believe are the most effective intervention strategies for helping students to overcome persistent literacy learning difficulties" (Tummer & Greaney, 2010, p. 229). For now, when working with children who appear to have dyslexia, we need to evaluate their strong or weak use of many types of strategies across various reading tasks (Johnson, 1995). Teachers must make a distinction between a *response to intervention* in an individualized and meaningful manner versus a *response to a program* for children like Elise, Natalie, and Joshua.

Definitions and operationalizations of learning disabilities and dyslexia are open-ended enough to label just about any child who is struggling in reading. Reid and Valle (2004) noted that the consequences of legitimizing dualisms in schools—"'normal' and 'abnormal,' 'able' and 'disabled'—as naturalized categories of individuals results in positioning students as either 'disabled' or 'nondisabled'" (p. 471). This mindset has dire consequences for children who are "struggling" to learn to read. The conventional wisdom of viewing children like Elise, Natalie, and Joshua as struggling, learning disabled, or dyslexic readers must be challenged. "When we consider that learning disabilities alone account for more than 50% of the population of special education students, we begin to see the proportions of the injustice" (Reid & Valle, 2004, p. 468). Maintaining current practices of making special education referrals, conducting intense observations, and administering a battery of psycho-educational tests continues to place problems within the individual child in a pathological manner. Furthermore, the injustice of this process is glaring because there isn't a single instructional program that teaches all children to read, and there are no clear definitions as to what constitutes true learning disabilities or dyslexia.

DISTINGUISHING ACHIEVEMENT GAPS VERSUS OPPORTUNITY GAPS

Elise, Natalie, and Joshua, considered "struggling readers," were referred for evaluation as possibly having a learning disorder. Elise was taught through a phonics program and became a letter-by-letter and word-by-word reader who lost meaning and pleasure in reading. Natalie was taught through a guided reading approach that emphasized comprehension conversations among members of her small group. As a result, she rarely had to confront the actual task of reading and showed little growth as a reader. Joshua was taught in small groups as well, but his teacher emphasized round-robin reading and oral accuracy, so he had little opportunity for discussion to develop his comprehension.

The Achievement Gap	The Opportunity Gap
Achievement gaps can occur when children like Elise, Natalie, and Joshua absorb the current instructional method for teaching reading with fidelity but have not achieved proficiency, fluency, and/or comprehension in a well-rounded manner.	The gap Elise, Natalie, and Joshua faced was not necessarily a result of a lack of reading instruction itself but rather a lack of reading instruction supporting their unique places of exploration. Instead of determining which of the students' skills were intact or deficient and supporting such skills, teachers referred the students to special education where they might be taught more isolated and fragmented skills and have less opportunity for authentic engagement in reading.

Because Elise, Natalie, and Joshua did not receive opportunities for well-rounded and authentic reading instruction, the result was an achievement gap unfairly justified by their teachers due to a possible cognitive or biological disability within each of them. It is entirely possible the fragmented reading instruction Elise, Natalie, and Joshua received may have actually caused their so-called "learning disabilities."

For most seasoned and fluent readers, reading seems automatic, especially if they learned to read at a young age without much difficulty. Even so, reading is a complex social, emotional, behavioral, linguistic, and cognitive process. "By the late 1990s, there was a sufficiently large body of basic research findings to forge a scientific consensus over the processes underlying skillful reading and the instructional practices that facilitated reading competence" (Kim, 2008, p. 373). Reading should be defined as a process of getting meaning from print, using knowledge about the written alphabet and about the sound structure of oral language for the purposes of achieving understanding (Snow, 1998). Proficient readers are flexible in using multiple strategies for decoding, obtaining meaning from words, and maintaining comprehension.

Knowing letter–sound relationships and recognizing words, left to right, line by line, from top to bottom, is paramount to the process of reading. However, exclusive teaching of phonics is only that—phonics as an isolated piece of the entire reading process. The concept of phonemic awareness began back in 1963 with Elkonin's (1963) assertion that "to learn to read, the child must be able to hear and distinguish the separate sounds in words" (p. 165). However, it may "seem justifiable to consider phonemic awareness a *cause* of reading acquisition, it may also be a *consequence* of reading acquisition" (Williams, 1995, p. 185; emphasis in the original). Research in past decades showed that proficient readers are flexible in using multiple strategies so they can concentrate on reading for meaning rather than decoding letter-by-letter and word-for-word. Ineffective readers tend to rely too heavily upon graphophonic cues (Routman, 1988). It is thought that proficient and fluent readers integrate three different cueing systems—(1) semantics (meaning), (2) syntactic (language structure), and (3) graphophonic (phonetic) cues—in a synchronized and meaningful manner. The three-cueing system is now most recognized in classroom practice as a way of teaching beginning readers to decode unknown words and comprehend text (Adams, 1998; Clay, 1993a; Routman, 1988).

Background knowledge and life experiences, spoken language, pragmatic (social) language, culture, priorities and purposes for reading, and genre, structure, and readability of text all have a substantial impact on an individual's reading experience at any point in time. These latter areas of impacts on reading are, by and large, not considered "issues" in a problematic and pathological sense but as the reality in which we tackle all kinds of print and online material in our literate society over a lifetime. Most students grow from reading itself—they learn new words, meanings, and concepts and read more books. However, although reading is best learned through reading, the serious caveat is that when "children find reading too difficult, they very often will not do it" (Adams, 1998, p. 73). Therefore, everyone from 9 months old to 9 years old to 90 years old could be viewed as being in different places in their exploration of language and literacy, including word recognition and automaticity, as opposed to having "struggles" with learning to read. When educators work from a broader and more positive viewpoint on literacy development and see that reading is indeed a complex, integrative, and dynamic process, opportunities for teaching and learning become meaningful and holistic.

Now, with scientific consensus that proficient and fluent readers use multiple strategies for both decoding and maintaining comprehension, researchers are asserting that "most reading difficulties can be prevented" (Snow, 1998, p. 13). Although there may be a range of rates of learning among students, "basic reading . . . is within the reach of every child. The key is good first teaching" (Fountas & Pinnell, 1996, p. 1). Some students may need a safety net, such as short-term but effective intervention, but "in order to prevent early struggles with literacy learning, we should be trying to understand the strategies the child is using" (Clay, 1993b, p. 4). There is no need to resort to unproductive uses of paraprofessionals, computer-based instructional programs, core reading programs, grade retention, segregated remediation programs, special education, and even disciplinary policies. Unfortunately, while the research field has reached a consensus, schools are holding on to conventional wisdom, tradition, dogma, and fads as vestiges of the deficit model of education and the reading wars. "The good news is that we now have an essential research base demonstrating that virtually every child could be reading on grade level by the end of first grade. The bad news is that almost no schools in the United States have anything in place that much looks like what the research says young children need to become engaged readers" (Allington, 2013, p. 520). Students who were not provided with good teaching, either through general education or short-term and effective intervention programs, may consequently be unjustifiably labeled as "struggling," "learning disabled," or "dyslexic." When teachers take ownership in providing high-quality instruction or leadership in coordinating well-matched interventions, the educational impact on students as having or thought as having disabilities is minimized.

Teachers are familiar with wide-ranging literacy experiences and the varying levels of reading abilities children bring to school. Almost every classroom has a child who is "struggling" with reading like Elise, Natalie, and Joshua. However, "the struggling reader label is socially constructed from students' relationship with their teachers and fellow students and their performance in meeting the standards of achievement of the schools' reading curriculum" (Risko & Walker-Dalhouse, 2012, p. 87). Taking on a viewpoint that all children are in a place of exploration as opposed to "struggling" has the potential to reduce opportunity gaps. "It is, therefore, incumbent on us to work diligently to learn how to implement inclusion well, both in our classrooms and in our professional discourses" (Reid & Valle, 2004, p. 468). People often joke that the weather being reported on the evening news doesn't match what's going on right outside the window. It's not a joke, however, when it comes to children learning how to read. Checking the weather outside the window is akin to closely observing students for their unique place in the exploration of literacy. It is essential for teachers, especially those in early childhood and elementary schools, to know what proficient and fluent reading entails and how to help children become stronger readers no matter where they are.

CHANGING THE TRAJECTORY OF CHILDREN VIEWED AS "STRUGGLING"

Because Elise, Natalie, and Joshua were "struggling" with reading, there was concern among their teachers that they might have a learning disability, language impairment, childhood depression, or even an ADD/ADHD. If we were to change the trajectory in their educational career, we would begin by placing ourselves, as their teachers, in a position to see where they are coming from as readers. We would be able to see that they were motivated and disciplined children who absorbed the current instructional method with conformity and commitment, yet the instructional method that had been imposed on them was unable to address their specific needs.

Not only do students have culturally, linguistically, and even "academically" diverse life experiences, but teachers need to see that all students are in unique places in their exploration of literacies and skills in learning to read and write. By adjusting our viewpoint, we can begin to see that all children desire to learn to read proficiently and fluently. Teachers can flexibly restructure their guided reading groups and instructional methods in order to ensure growth. "The teacher has a unique opportunity to intervene in the narrative of the struggling reader. Before engaging with a struggling reader—or any reader—it is imperative that a teacher believes that *every* child can learn and can contribute to the learning community" (Vlach & Burcie, 2010, p. 522). Teachers only need to see their students' unique place as a positive place, as a place in the right direction. Therefore, when "arranging literacy environments that provide opportunities for all students to be contributing members of the class, teachers can offer struggling readers both individualized instruction and full membership in the class community" (Vlach & Burcie, 2010, p. 523).

In designing a flexible and inclusive classroom filled with language and literacies so all children are participating members of the learning community, there would be no need to arbitrarily excuse children from a specific task or to recommend them for special education or intervention because they don't seem able to access the literacy curriculum. Excusing or removing them from regular class only fills children's narratives with rejection and inadequacy, and does not engage struggling readers, thus denying them equal rights and membership in their classroom (Vlach & Burcie, 2010). Opportunities for inclusive and differentiated instruction within the classroom can be provided and outside intervention can be used only as a last resort or, at least, in a manner that is aligned, purposeful, and effective. A fully inclusive classroom is where Elise, who was first taught through a prescribed phonics program, can begin to read for fluency and pleasure. It is one in which Natalie, who has a strong ability to carry on conversations about books, could improve word recognition skills so that she can read on her own. And it is one where Joshua, who is adept at oral reading, could be given plenty of silent-reading opportunities and book-club conversations to strengthen his comprehension. All three children, among their peers and with guidance from teachers, can thrive in an environment where connections among language, reading, and writing are made and where they are able to show off their reading strengths as well as address their weaknesses. Teachers may ask themselves the following questions as they move toward eliminating gaps in educational opportunity.

All Children Are Explorers of Literacies

What does your inner voice say about a student who is "struggling" with reading? Listen to it carefully. How can you ensure opportunities for learning to read and strengthening literacy in an authentic and purposeful manner?

When teachers redefine the concept of "struggling" to see that all children are in different places in their exploration of language and literacies, they are in a better position to bridge what children know with academic literacy in a formal school environment. There is lack of consensus as to what constitutes learning disabilities, dyslexia, and other reading "disorders." The terms are variously seen as different from or synonymous with several other labels that involve problems with literacy (Elliott & Grigorenko, 2014). Instead of making broad attempts to define, assess, and make diagnoses and forming pathological viewpoints toward students, teachers can work to offer flexible guided reading groups, provide individual and meaningful lessons, set aside time for shared and independent reading, and ensure that there are plentiful opportunities for students to strengthen their literacy alongside their peers. When general education teachers use strong leadership and supervision, they certainly can recruit reading intervention teachers and other personnel to provide short-term, closely aligned, and purposeful support in individual or small-group literacy instruction. When students are viewed as explorers of language and literacy through the use of close observations and running records, teachers have healthier opportunities to know and encourage students as growing readers and writers.

The Power of Running Records

Do you know what each of your students specifically needs to grow in reading? What do students do when stuck on an unknown word? How is their fluency? Is it smooth, with good inflection, or is it halting, word-by-word reading? Is there depth

to comprehension conversation following reading? Are they
making any personal connections to text? Are there issues with
attention, stamina, and motivation while reading? Has your
students' visual acuity been checked? What kinds of books does
each student like to read?

Teachers who provide high-quality reading lessons are not experts on specific intervention methods or programs, but they are "experts" on the instructional needs of the individuals at hand. Though knowledge about various approaches for teaching reading is important, the power of running records should not be underestimated. The most effective way to understand what a child like Elise, Natalie, or Joshua knows about the reading process is to take a running record. Running records refer to the process of observing a child reading aloud a short passage and later analyzing both accuracy and the types of errors made in order to determine which cueing strategies the child may or may not be using. It is a multidimensional assessment that allows teachers to gather observational and quantitative data on a reader's performance that are reliable, useful, and efficient (Shea, 2012). Running records are an excellent mechanism for teachers to become experts on an individual child's instructional needs as opposed to being an expert on a particular reading program or two and arbitrarily implementing these programs in classrooms.

Even though "running records are used as a benchmark or standards-based reading assessment across grade levels in elementary schools" (Fawson, Ludlow, Reutzel, Sudweeks, & Smith, 2006, p. 113), their original purpose was to assess a child's reading behavior by examining both accuracy and types of errors and self-corrections during oral reading in order to guide instructional decisions (Clay, 1993a). Running records are a tool for observing and informing literacy instruction whereas benchmarking tends to be used as an assessment for the sole purpose of leveling and grouping students. Analyzing running records from readers who are "struggling" as well as readers who are proficient and fluent both provides professional development for teachers on the reading development continuum and places care and thought into children's unique needs in their exploration of literacies and learning to read and write, no matter what their "levels" are.

Taking Back Ownership and Leadership

Are you taking ownership—and leadership—in mobilizing support
staff such as reading intervention teachers, reading coaches, in-
class parent and community volunteers, and guest readers without
simply passing children who are "struggling" on to someone else?

Too often, children who are found "struggling" based on district or state-wide assessment scores are arbitrarily placed into a separate remedial reading program. Because Elise, Natalie, and Joshua were at different places in their exploration of literacy, it would not help them to be placed into a similar remedial reading program. However, individualized, short-term, and intensive intervention might be beneficial. When teachers have intimate knowledge of their students' literacies, through running records, observations, and guided reading groups, they are in the best position to ensure cohesive learning experiences. Opportunities for students occur when teachers take ownership and leadership because of this knowledge. Therefore, support professionals such as reading intervention teachers, Title I teachers, special education teachers and therapists, English language learning teachers, and paraprofessionals avoid operating in a vacuum. Because "placing at-risk students in two or more different reading curricula would have a less positive effect on student achievement than simply personalizing, extending, and intensifying the reading instruction offered in the classroom reading lessons" (Allington, 2006, p. 20), close collaboration and coordination among all team members is of utmost importance. "Educators have a special responsibility to teach every child and not to blame children, families, or each other when the task is difficult. All responsible adults need to work together to help children become competent readers and writers" (Neuman, Copple, & Bredekamp, 2000, p. 19). Taking ownership and leadership ensures coordination for children's true opportunities to learn to read proficiently and fluently.

Ensuring Opportunities for Reading Engagement

How can you ensure your students are partaking of a well-rounded, authentic literacy curriculum, including read-aloud time, shared reading, independent reading, guided reading, writing, and word work?

Engaged readers are described as motivated to read, strategic in their approaches to comprehending what they read, knowledgeable in their construction of meaning from text, and socially interactive while reading (Guthrie, Wigfield, & You, 2012). Several studies (Allington, 2002; Brenner, Hiebert, & Tompkins, 2009; Gambrell, 2011) found that in many elementary classrooms, children spent only 10 to 20 minutes per day actually *reading*. This is despite having allocated time for reading instruction ranging from 90 to 120 minutes per day. "Even in a time when policies mandate an increase in the amount of time spent on reading instruction, the time that students spend in reading texts has not increased substantially from earlier eras. Further, lessons in and practice on particular skills and subskills of reading do not necessarily translate into a habit of engaged reading over a lifetime" (Hiebert, 2009, p. ix). Focusing on opportunities for children to *read* in the school environment is crucial. Therefore, teachers are wise to objectively clock how much *time* students actually *engage* in *real* reading (and writing) at school, with or without adult support, on a daily basis.

Reading proficiency and fluency are not likely to increase if 90 minutes or more are devoted to reading instruction but that instruction is consumed with trivial tasks, such as lessons in or practice on sub-skills of reading. (Hiebert, 2009). Time spent on "seatwork" is particularly problematic for children who are identified for special education services. "We know that active involvement in actual reading and writing of texts is critical to accelerated development, yet remedial and special education students are the group least likely to be asked to read or write—in any sustained form—during instruction" (Walmsley & Allington, 1995, p. 23). Teachers can minimize the use of flash cards, worksheets, and phonics-based software by providing meaningful instruction and practice on the use of skills within authentic texts.

Widespread public campaigns to encourage independent reading at home have occurred for decades and continue today, but how much children read at home is beyond schools' control. Ultimately, if children are not reading at school, and if they are also not reading at home, then opportunities for them to become proficient and fluent readers simply do not exist. Therefore, teachers should actively seek opportunities for students to comfortably settle in with a book, perhaps on the floor or in a beanbag chair, or even as one of the rotations in literacy centers.

Managing Influences of Parents and Community Members

How can you advocate for a reading curriculum that is authentic, open-ended, engaging, and embraces a culturally and linguistically diverse population?

Just as in the metaphor of meteorology, where everyone is an expert on weather, parents, community members, administrators, and politicians may attempt to use power and funds to influence how the reading curriculum should be implemented in their local schools. Many reading instruction products—complete with materials, workbooks, and even technological tools and software—make hefty claims in their effectiveness in teaching reading. People with little or no expertise in the processes of reading or literacy development can be easily swayed by promotional material. However, legislators and policymakers must understand the complex role of teachers in providing reading instruction, because some children—like Elise, Natalie, and Joshua, who are not progressing on any one program— may very well end up being viewed as "struggling," "learning disabled," or "dyslexic." Teachers who make clear they are bridging multiple language and literacies, and not reducing standards or enabling children, become good advocates for themselves as professionals and for their children as individuals. In doing do so, they garner support for a flexible, responsive, and opportunistic reading curriculum that supports the exploration of literacy among all children.

NO MATTER THE WEATHER

As shown in this chapter, the labeling of children as "struggling," "learning disabled," or "dyslexic" is something that is socially and politically constructed by the adults around them, often depending on the current "weather" in a school or district. For as long as we preserve special education as a separate entity in the face of increasing diversity, and with it the groundless and often biased division between "normal" and "disabled," vicious cycles of underachievement are likely to continue for the children who receive these labels. Such dualistic labeling allows educators to continue practices of insidious segregation within their classrooms and schools. However, general education teachers are in a prime position to change this state of our schools by insisting on a climate of inclusion for all learners and by viewing reading differences from an understanding that all children are in different places in their exploration of language and literacies over their life spans. Because reading is a complex, integrative, and dynamic process, we can no longer retain a narrow scope of pedagogy in which only a select group of children can achieve.

CHAPTER 3

The Gift of Reading

THE GAP:
ABLEISM TOWARD STUDENTS IN "SPECIAL EDUCATION"

Adam, a student with cerebral palsy, had an unsteady gait when walking. One of his wrists was curled in so tightly that he used a brace. Thus, matching words with his finger as he learned to read and using an eraser as a source of stickiness to turn pages made his reading fluency a labor. Annie, who had spent much time in hospitals and recovery because of severe scoliosis, used a slant board so that books were tilted up for her to read. She suffered from fatigue and took frequent naps throughout her school day. Mike, who had muscular dystrophy, was in a wheelchair and was unable to physically hold books. However, he did enjoy reading from a laptop computer with a touchpad.

Parker had been diagnosed with fetal alcohol syndrome and Shelly had Down syndrome. Their general intellectual functioning was significantly lower than the average for their chronological age. Cognitive impairments or developmental disabilities can result from chromosomal abnormalities or genetic syndromes, maternal alcohol or substance abuse during the pregnancy, complications during birth, infections the mother might have during the pregnancy or the baby might acquire in early life, or exposure to high levels of environmental toxins. (Centers for Disease Control and Prevention, 2014). Despite their disabilities, both Parker and Shelly loved listening to and looking at picture books and pointing at the items in the illustrations.

Madison, who had an autism spectrum disorder, was able to read words by rote with nearly perfect accuracy several grade levels above her peers, yet her precocious decoding ability masked her issues with comprehension. Marcus suffered frequent seizures and health problems for most of his preschool years. No one knew for sure what kind of damage his brain had sustained from these seizures. Despite his swollen gums and impaired speech, he demonstrated comprehension of the books that he read through his sense of humor and affection for ironic endings in books by using his big smiles and exuberant body language. Abby had not spoken a word during her first few days at school. Days led to weeks, and she was still not speaking, leading her teachers to believe that she had apraxia or mutism. She would only nod or shake her head and point at things. Nevertheless, it was obvious that she understood others around her, and as a result, was behaving appropriately and doing what she was supposed to be doing. Storytime appeared to be her favorite part of the school day.

All of these students with disabilities, from kindergarten to 4th grade, were placed in Mr. Lee's resource room for the morning every day. Each received various speech and language, occupational, and physical therapies and social work services in between opportunities to attend music and art classes and recess with their typically developing peers throughout the afternoon. These eight students demonstrate a huge range of abilities and needs, but were all assigned to the same special education classroom, in which they had very little time for participation in a general education literacy curriculum. They illustrate the incredible diversity of students who are being served by special education. The purpose of special education is to meet the individual education needs of students with disabilities as well as make sure that they are educated alongside nondisabled peers to the maximum extent appropriate (U.S. Department of Education, 2010). Yet, students in special education have just as varied individual literacy needs as students in a general education classroom, except their opportunities for language and literacy growth is limited by their perceived incapableness. And they are limited by the lack of exposure to a full range of engaging and rich language and literacy opportunities in a diverse classroom.

PROBLEMS WITH PLACING STUDENTS IN "SPECIAL EDUCATION"

All of these children in Mr. Lee's resource room, who had a wide range of conditions from mild to severe stemming from either congenital or hereditary causes, were designated "special education" students. The diverse and sometimes ill-defined reasons for students being arbitrarily assigned to separate special education classrooms can set them up for a significant opportunity gap in their educational career by causing educators to make assumptions about limits to children's intelligence or ability that may or may not be true. Some students are diagnosed with a learning disability or dyslexia because of their unexplained and unexpected reasons for underachievement in literacy. Others have medically identified disabilities that are too often erroneously explained as reasons for underachievement in literacy. No one—not even experienced special educators and educational psychologists—knows the full capabilities of a particular student unless that student is given an opportunity to learn in a general education curriculum with accommodations. Therefore, students' participation as fully accepted members of general education classrooms would expose them to the curriculum and the real world and also increase their chances of demonstrating learning with their fullest capabilities. Not only that, but their participation would expose their peers to the diversity that exists among all of us, creating a climate of inclusivity and acceptance for all.

Many general education teachers do not feel they are well trained to teach students with disabilities, so they think that these students would be better educated elsewhere, such as in resource rooms or special education classrooms. An issue dividing special and general teachers is the meaning they attach to the "dis" in the word *disabilities*. "Equating disability with deficits firmly situates learning problems in the minds and bodies of individual students, which is, of course, consistent with the disciplinary roots of special education in medicine and behavioral psychology" (Cochran-Smith & Dudley-Marling, 2012, p. 240). This viewpoint, often held by both special and general education teachers, sees remediating, rehabilitating, or otherwise overcoming disabilities so students can access academic instruction as a responsibility limited to trained special educators and therapists. However, although the laws currently in place are designed to protect the rights of students with disabilities, customize their education, and provide accommodations, only 11% of 4th-grade students and 9% of 8th-grade students with disabilities performed at or above the *Proficient* level in reading in 2013 (National Center for Education Statistics, 2013). Even though most teachers and administrators agree with Wei, Blackorby, and Schiller (2011) that *"students with disabilities*, as a subgroup under NCLB, is simply too heterogeneous to fairly evaluate a school's efforts to improve student performance" (p. 102), such students' low rate of achievement still makes them one of the most underserved populations in reading instruction. Their low rate of reading achievement, however, is not the sole responsibility of special versus general education teachers. Rather, their underachievement occurs because of the systemic structure of our schools. Both special and general education teachers can work collaboratively to ensure that students with disabilities are full members of a general education classroom and that they have complete access to the language and literacy curriculum.

THE COSTS AND BENEFITS OF SPECIAL EDUCATION

Just a generation or two ago, states continued to enact statutes that specifically authorized school officials to exclude students with disabilities from public education (Yell, Rogers, & Rogers, 1988, p. 220). By 1975, the Education for All Handicapped Children Act (EHA) was enacted with the intention of preserving the educational rights of students with disabilities. The EHA required all schools to provide equal access to education for students with physical and mental disabilities in the least restrictive environments. Schools were required to conduct evaluations and create an educational plan documenting how students, like those in Mr. Lee's resource room, can be allowed an educational experiences that mirrors as closely as possible the experiences of students without disabilities.

The number of students between age 3 and 21 in special education is around 13% of the total public school enrollment (National Center for Education Statistics, 2010). Some of these students have a pathological or medical condition such as a hearing, visual, cognitive, or orthopedic impairment. Others are identified, usually through school systems, as having a speech and language impairment, learning disability, or emotional impairment, which may or may not necessarily be pathological in nature but may be socially and politically constructed by the schools. For many years, almost half of special education students were classified as having a specific learning disability as their primary disability (Aron & Loprest, 2012). No matter what reason is given for referring a student to special education, the designation often transfers responsibility for a specific student's education and chronic underachievement from general education to special education.

Although special education is intended to meet the atypical cognitive, emotional, behavioral, or physical needs of students with disabilities, therapeutic services and accommodations for these students are costly to schools. The ratio of current operating expenditures, excluding expenditures on school facilities, on the typical student in special education is 2.08 times what is spent on the typical student in regular education with no special needs (Chambers, Parrish, & Harr, 2004). Because the diagnostic process, which involves reviewing student records, assessing, evaluating, and documentating, is intensive, it places the lens on an individual student as having a disease, illness, or problem and leads to labeling of students. Viewing a disease, illness, or problem as the culprit behind learning difficulties in reading or writing too often leaves teachers and schools unaccountable for the students' academic achievement.

Once a student is identified as having a disability, Individualized Education Plans (IEPs) provide a continuum of services that range from using minimal accommodation in general education classrooms to resource rooms for part of the school day to separate, self-contained classrooms. Many students with disabilities, like the students in Mr. Lee's resource room, receive additional therapeutic services such as speech and language therapy, physical or occupational therapy, counseling, and social work support. Schools may hire a paraprofessional to work with a child with disabilities in his or her general education classroom. Though federal laws require that students with disabilities be placed in the least restrictive educational environment possible, what is considered *least restrictive* is subjective. Arguing for or against the amount of inclusion in a general education classroom versus a resource room or self-contained classroom with regard to access to the curriculum has been and continues to be a contentious and even litigious process among parents, teachers, special educators and therapists, and administrators.

Several amendments and changes to special education policies have been made throughout the years since the original passage of the EHA. A notable change was the 1990 amendment that renamed the law the Individuals with Disabilities Act (IDEA) in order to emphasize children as children first by removing the term *handicapped*. A vast majority of students in special education (80%–85%) can meet the same achievement standards as other students if they are given specially designed instruction, appropriate access, supports, and accommodations, as required by the IDEA (Thurlow, Quenemoen, & Lazarus, 2013). Unfortunately, many students with disabilities are offered therapies and even lessons on self-care and life skills, including rudimentary literacy such as reading signs on restroom doors and the symbol for poison, instead of true educational opportunities for strengthening deeper language and literacy.

Not only is special education financially costly for schools, but it can also be costly for individual students (Hibel, Farkas, & Morgan, 2010). Despite special educators' best intentions to help students live and learn to their fullest capabilities, teacher and administrator mindsets continue to distinguish between what is "normal" and "abnormal." For the unfortunate students who fall into the abnormal categories, even if they have normal cognitive and language abilities to think, reason, and problem-solve, they may be subjected to covert segregation, lower expectations, and reading programs that lack solid evidence of effectiveness.

Although recognition of individual differences is a cornerstone of special education, in many cases, as in Mr. Lee's resource room, all special education students receive the same cookie-cutter IEPs and "blanket" programs, which may or may not meet the needs of individual students (Keogh, 2007). The appearance of opportunity in the form of special education is often not the reality.

DISTINGUISHING ACHIEVEMENT GAPS VERSUS OPPORTUNITY GAPS

The students on Mr. Lee's caseload were identified as being in need of special education and all were reading below grade level. All were placed in a single resource room and instructed in the same phonics-based online reading program for 90 minutes per day. Three paraprofessionals were available to help them type and maneuver the mouse on their computers. The paraprofessionals were also on hand to manage frequent meltdowns due to frustration, resistance, and even boredom. All of the students were viewed as having a condition—a disease, illness, or problem—that was the primary reason for their difficulties in learning to read and write at the same level as their nondisabled peers. However, the first three students—Adam, Annie, and Mike—had only physical or health impairments that impacted their ability to physically hold books and pencils, turn pages and write or type, and read or write in reasonable comfort. Even though reading and writing was a cumbersome physical process for them, they did not have any sort of language or cognitive incapability to become literate and attain a high level of educational achievement. In contrast, Parker and Shelly both had developmental disabilities that impacted both their cognitive and language functioning. Their educational needs may be more significant than the students with physical disabilities alone, and they may need additional accommodations. Whether or not all students with developmental disabilities develop literacy abilities on a similar timetable or demonstrate the same outcomes as their nondisabled peers, access to high-quality literacy instruction holds immediate and lifelong benefits. The evidence is growing that students with developmental disabilities, including children like Parker and Shelly, can develop meaningful literacy abilities when they have access to evidence-based instruction and rich literacy classrooms (Schnorr, 2011). Furthermore, the utmost care must be taken to avoid making assumptions about students' cognitive, or intellectual, functioning. Some students, like Madison, Marcus, and Abby, may appear to be "slow" when in fact they are only facing challenges in their ability to communicate effectively in a social and verbal manner. Making a broad assumption about a student's intelligence or ability has the potential to set that student up for a significant opportunity gap and provide him or her with only a limited educational experience. There is very little reason why most students can't be provided literacy instruction in general education classrooms alongside their nondisabled peers.

The Achievement Gap	The Opportunity Gap
Achievement gaps can occur when the disabilities of students become the main focus in their educational career. A vicious cycle of underachievement occurs when significant amounts of time are spent on various therapies and in resource rooms in order to "help" students become part of the educational community. These students almost never have the opportunity to "catch up" with their general education peers with regard to their literacy development and academic achievement.	The gap that students identified as having special education needs faced was not necessarily a result of their disabilities but rather was because of few or a lack of opportunities for literacy instruction, regardless of their educational placement. Too often, attitudes toward their disabilities— more so than the disabilities themselves—have a major impact on the literacy development and education these students receive.

"Often in schools, the onus for participation is placed on the child. That is, the child must perform at a particular academic level or behave in an acceptable way to access appropriate education"(Hehir, 2005, p. 45). Most people would agree that reading is the foundation to a good educational outcome; however, resource room services and therapies work toward narrow goals pertaining to their specific fields, as in speech, physical, or occupational therapy, without a tight and common goal of making sure students learn to read proficiently and write effectively and ultimately receive a quality education.

Ableism is discrimination in favor of people who are able-bodied as well as prejudice against or disregard of the needs of people with disabilities. Not unlike racism, ableism is subtle and pervasive in our schools and the larger society. "Progress toward equity is dependent first and foremost on the acknowledgement that ableism exists in schools" (Hehir, 2005, p. 17). Though the term *ableism* (or any other *ism*, for that matter) usually elicits a defensive response that undermines trust among those working in diverse environments, it is crucial for teachers to unlearn unconscious ableist patterns of thinking. To understand the roots of ableism, we need to learn to see how "most people go through life being judged for what they *can* do, whereas people with identified disabilities are usually first seen through a lens of what they *cannot* do" (Ramsey, 2004, p. 141). Ableist views insist that anyone who is disabled is abnormal and must somehow *overcome* or *cure* their impairment or differences first in order to be educated and accepted as part of mainstream society.

Ableism aside, many teachers are willing to include students with disabilities, but they raise many valid questions and concerns. They fear they are not trained to work with students with particular disabilities or health issues, such as Adam's cerebral palsy, Shelly's Down syndrome, or Madison's autism spectrum disorder. Teachers worry that certain students' disabilities will divert attention from other students. In this heightened political climate of standardized testing, there is also worry that students with disabilities will bring down overall class averages and cause their teachers to be deemed ineffective. Districts that provide a one-size-fits-all reading curriculum make it difficult for teachers to embrace and foster diversity in classrooms. Further compounding the situation, teachers have little training in reading diagnosis and instruction, whereas special education teachers, who have much training in a specific disability area, have little training in reading as well. This hyper-specialized structure is an issue in attempts to provide differentiation for *all* students, whether they have identified disabilities or not.

When a disability becomes the main focus of a student's education, a significant amount of time is spent on various therapies to help that student become part of the educational community. All of the students with disabilities on Mr. Lee's caseload found themselves in speech therapy, physical therapy, occupational therapy, and social work sessions, and were also removed from their general education classrooms for academic support in Mr. Lee's resource room in order to "catch up." They miss out on authentic and meaningful reading (and other academic) instruction as a result of the time they spend on various therapies; interestingly, some students—like Adam (cerebral palsy) and Marcus (seizures)—ended up receiving private tutoring at home because they were lagging so far behind academically.

Decisions in special education for students with disabilities are too often made on beliefs and hope. Some widely used methods are questionable, even controversial, and are based on beliefs and advocacy rather than on documentation of their effectiveness (Keogh, 2007, p. 68). When teachers, administrators, and parents make placement and instructional decisions for students in special education, they usually do so on the basis of existing programs, available accommodations, or even the prevailing educational philosophy. Without any kind of systemic and progress monitoring toward curriculum standards and outcomes for individuals in special education, true opportunities for learning and achievement may be lost.

Even students with disabilities who currently spend a large portion of their days in a general education classroom under the guise of "inclusion" may not receive direct and consistent instruction from the general education teacher or may otherwise not be fully accessing the curriculum. They may be subjected to lower expectations than their peers, through a modified and watered-down curriculum, such as having simplified or adjusted rubrics for writing or extended timelines for research projects. They may have well-meaning paraprofessionals following, explaining, or even doing unnecessary things for them. Some paraprofessionals become the teachers themselves, providing students with separate assignments on a separate table or in the hallway. Inclusion is not inclusion if students with disabilities are placed in general education in body only.

CHANGING THE TRAJECTORY OF STUDENTS IN "SPECIAL EDUCATION"

All of the students in Mr. Lee's resource room, who exhibited a wide range of individual capabilities and accommodations, were functioning below age- and grade-level norms in literacy development and academic achievement. Because they were all identified as "special education students," they were expected to underachieve. To change their trajectory, teachers would first need to see them as fully capable of becoming strong readers and writers. Even students with serious cognitive delays can be viewed as more capable of participating in literacy instruction than might once have been envisioned. By adjusting teachers' viewpoints, we can begin to see that most students with disabilities (as opposed to only a few who somehow "overcome" their disabilities) are fully capable of learning to read proficiently and fluently and of belonging in general education classrooms with their nondisabled peers. With this new viewpoint, general education teachers can take ownership for ensuring that *all* students have access to high-quality literacy instruction that includes hearing adults read aloud, shared reading among peers, independent reading, and small-group guided reading lessons, along with an assortment of word work and writing activities. General education teachers can use the support of special education and intervention teachers so that accommodations and literacy instruction can be restructured to include all students. With the help of a committed general classroom teacher, students with special needs can regularly receive the message that their learning is the responsibility of every educator with whom they come into contact, not just the specialists (Walmsley & Allington, 1995).

Instead of somehow making students with disabilities ready for literacy instruction in a general education classroom, classrooms—designed through the collaboration of both general and special educators along with administrators and other support professionals—can be made ready for students, as they come, as the first step in closing opportunity gaps. We should begin with the student behind the disability first: Students come with a wide range of literacy experiences, from their homes, from school, from their environment, just like their nondisabled peers. We can change our thinking from what they *can't*, *won't*, or are *too low in their reading levels* to do to a line of thinking where we ask: What *can* we do? What *can* the student do? How do we start? How do we include the student as a viable member of the classroom?

Because teachers are in the central position of offering a variety of approaches for teaching reading, continually assessing students' individual progress, and ensuring opportunities for engaged reading, they are in the best position to do all this for students with disabilities as well. Although truly inclusive schools are few and far between, teachers can certainly begin to develop inclusive classrooms and encourage their colleagues to do the same. The O'Hearn Elementary School in Boston (since renamed Dr. William W. Henderson K–12 Inclusion School) provides an example of a truly inclusive model, in which students with and without disabilities all learn together in inclusive classrooms. Approximately 30% of the students at Henderson School have disabilities. Each classroom, with approximately 22 students, typically contains about 15 students without disabilities, four with significant disabilities, and three or four with mild or moderate disabilities. The school uses a workshop approach, meaning that students start most lessons as a large group for a short presentation or "mini-lesson." Students spend most of their time doing activities, and there were many opportunities for teachers to support and challenge students individually and in small groups at appropriate skill levels. After each lesson is finished, the students share their learning with their peers. Under the guidance of the school's principal, Dr. William Henderson (who happens to be blind, and who introduced this inclusive model), the academic performance of all students has risen significantly. Henderson remarked that including students with a range of disabilities became the catalyst for transforming general education at the school; in fact, including disabled students helped general education teachers figure out how to improve teaching and learning for everyone (Henderson, 2011).

When a general education teacher makes reflective changes to the curriculum or instructional methods to accommodate students with disabilities, *all* the students in that classroom will benefit greatly. These kinds of changes are characterized as *universal design*. First coined in architecture, universal design is an approach in which products and environments are designed to be as usable by as many people as possible, regardless of age, ability, or situation. For example, switching from doorknobs to handles makes it much easier for young children's hands, older arthritic hands, and even adult hands carrying bags of groceries to open. In education, Universal Design for Learning (UDL) refers to a process by which a curriculum (i.e., goals, methods, materials, and assessments) is intentionally and systematically designed from the beginning to address individual differences. With curricula that are designed according to the principles of UDL, the difficulties and expenses of subsequent "retrofitting" and adaptation of "disabled" curricula can be reduced or eliminated—and a better learning environment can be implemented. It provides flexibility in the ways information is presented, in the ways students respond or demonstrate knowledge and skills, and in the ways students are engaged. It also reduces barriers in instruction; provides appropriate accommodations, supports, and challenges; and maintains high achievement expectations for all students, including those with disabilities (National Center on Universal Design for Learning, 2014).

When students with disabilities are not presented to others around them in a patronizing or stereotypical manner, in such a way that they are referred to as "special," their participation becomes merely a matter of diversity. Recognition of disability as a basic diversity issue—that disability is not to be pitied, patronized, or vilified—is important in helping disabled students feel comfortable with their disability and progress well in schools (Hehir, 2005). Teachers may ask themselves the following questions as they move toward eliminating gaps in educational opportunity for students with disabilities:

Remembering the Student Behind the Disability

What does your inner voice about students needing special education say? Listen to it carefully. Are you looking at the disability first or the student first? Are you avoiding looking at what the student can't do, as opposed to what the student can do? How can you contribute to the student's education in a proactive and positive manner?

Of course, we need to acknowledge impairments in order to remove barriers and provide accommodations, but we mustn't forget the *student* behind the disability. Students with disabilities, just like their general education peers, come to school with a wide range of literacy experiences and a desire to learn to read and write. When teachers see that even students with disabilities—most of whom can meet the same achievement standards as their nondisabled peers—are students first, they can also see that students with disabilities too, are at different places in their exploration of language and literacies. It is irresponsible to assume that because a student receives special education services, that student is a low performer who cannot learn (Thurlow, Quenemoen, & Lazarus, 2013). Furthermore, educators must ensure that the provision of special education services doesn't compromise a student's education. For example, providing physical therapy for Adam because he has cerebral palsy shouldn't hamper his access to a challenging literacy curriculum, where his above-average intelligence will serve him well in his future educational and career endeavors. The concept of universal design in education can broaden the literacy experience for all students. As with students who were previously considered "unready" or "struggling" in reading or writing, teachers can get to know and accept disabled students as individuals in a positive manner and use a variety of approaches to support them as growing readers and writers.

Ensuring Opportunities for Reading Engagement

Are there areas where you, as a teacher, can adapt your presentation or provide accommodations so that students with disabilities can thrive as engaged readers and writers and participate in a challenging curriculum with their nondisabled peers?

Students with disabilities learn at their fullest capabilities when they are surrounded by general education peers in an inclusive environment. Universally designed schools and programs that consider the needs of disabled students from their inception can greatly increase opportunities for the integration of students with disabilities while minimizing the impact of their disabilities on their education (Hehir, 2005). Many teachers schedule a large block of time for literacy development, one that includes opportunities for listening to a teacher read aloud, shared reading, guided reading, independent reading, shared writing, interactive writing, writer's workshop, independent writing, and word work (Fountas & Pinnell, 1996). The concept of universal design, if well organized and managed, is already inherent in this literacy framework. Even within the framework of existing school structures or literacy programs, teachers can find ways to universally design their own classrooms and support inclusivity for all students by making teaching materials and centers flexible and open-ended. All the students on Mr. Lee's caseload are fully capable of partaking in each of these literacy lessons or centers when their environment is set up from the beginning to support literacy exploration for all students, whether they have disabilities or not.

Taking Back Ownership and Leadership

*Are you taking ownership—and leadership—in mobilizing the
special education team without simply passing the disabled
student off to them? How are you accepting educational
accountability for your students? How are you keeping the
special education team informed of each student's participation
and literacy progress in the general education classroom?*

Students with disabilities most often have written accommodations and modifications on their Individualized Education Plans (IEPs). Because general education teachers are required to be a member of the IEP team (United States Department of Education, 2006b), it is important to distinguish between accommodations and modifications. *Accommodations* are specific supports put in place to help students overcome or work around their disabilities. They do not change the standards or expectations, but they do allow students to strive to meet these challenges. Adam, with his tightly curled wrist, could read in his guided reading group from a tablet with an e-book loaded on to it. Abby, who did not speak, was able to rearrange cut-up sentences and point to words and concepts she knows at a center with her peers. *Modifications*, on the other hand, change the standards through an altered form of instruction or assessment and should be used only with extreme caution because they may turn out to limit opportunities for students with disabilities. For example, Parker and Shelly, who have developmental disabilities, may need some modifications in their instruction and assessment, particularly if they are far below age and grade norms. However, as members of their general education classroom, they are exposed to the curriculum and the real world. Using educational standards, such as the Common Core State Standards (CCSS), as guidelines, close collaboration and coordination among the various therapists and special educators, with the general education teacher taking the lead, is of utmost importance in reducing opportunity gaps for students with disabilities.

Monitoring Individual Growth

*How will you know if your student is making growth in reading?
In what ways and how often will you assess your student's
progress in reading?*

Students with disabilities should have their individual growth in reading and writing closely monitored in order to provide meaningful and effective instructional guidance and scaffolding, just as is done with their general education peers. Even though many schools require reading assessments only two or three times per year, much growth (or lack of growth) occurs between these time frames. Students may use accommodations when being assessed; when documenting observations, taking running records, or using standardized assessment tools, it is appropriate to indicate the provision of accommodations on protocol forms for students with disabilities. Monitoring students' reading from their full language and cognitive capabilities, as opposed to their pathological condition, goes a long way toward ensuring continued growth.

Setting Clear Boundaries for Paraprofessionals or Teacher Assistants

Are you setting clear boundaries for the paraprofessionals or teacher assistants in your classroom? How can you ensure that you, as the general education teacher, are taking full responsibility for the student's education while making use of the help of these professionals?

There are many paraprofessionals who maintain clear boundaries between general education teachers, themselves, and the students to whom they were assigned. Some serve solely as sign language interpreters. Some provide only physical assistance. Others, however, provide academic and social assistance, and this is where the boundaries get blurry. Too often, students and their parents look to the paraprofessional instead of the general education teacher for assistance, guidance, and even separate instruction. When paraprofessionals or teacher assistants do unnecessary things for students with disabilities, these students get very little opportunity to develop independency, resiliency, and a sense of belonging. Strong communication between the general education and support staff ensures that students have full access to the general education teacher and the literacy curriculum.

Minding the Logistics of Schoolwide Literacy Events

Many literacy events, such as parent-teacher conferences, book fairs, or pajama nights, are often inaccessible or otherwise impractical for families who have a student with a disability. In what ways can you ensure there are adequate accommodations in place for the entire family to participate?

Schoolwide events such as parent-teacher conferences, book fairs, or pajama nights are planned with the best intention of bridging home–school partnerships. However, the logistics for families having a student with a disability to partake in these events may outweigh the benefits of attending, particularly if the student's condition is severe and requires specialized transportation or trained babysitters. General education teachers, along with their administrators, may want to rethink school events from the perspective of these families and take steps to minimize any obstacles to their participation. Making sure the entire building and schoolwide programs are universally designed from the beginning goes a long way toward increasing participation among all families.

DO WE REALLY NEED *SPECIAL* EDUCATION?

As long as schools, research communities, publishers, public policymakers, teacher unions, and the media are still operating on an ableist belief system that students with disabilities are in need of *special* education, which too often means that they are removed from the general classroom, they paradoxically create opportunity gaps. What these students really need is high expectations, inclusion, engagement, and a strong sense of their own capabilities. Therefore, individualized education should be offered in the form of universally designed instruction within the schools and general education classrooms. Special education teachers, interventionists, and therapists should provide technical assistance or install accommodations as necessary for students with disabilities and strive to seek how students can reach educational goals similar to those of their nondisabled peers. Small-group or individualized reading sessions outside of the classroom may be helpful to some students with disabilities, but these must closely align with the general education curriculum. Any form of literacy instruction, in or out of the classroom, should be authentic, meaningful, and purposeful. By recognizing that students—despite their disabilities or health issues—are students first and that they *can* learn to read, write, and become literate alongside their nondisabled peers and by catching our collective ableist voices, we can surely reduce the opportunity gaps for our "special education" population.

CHAPTER 4

It Looks Greek to Me

THE GAP:
REGARDING FORMS OF SPEECH AND ENGLISH AS "NONSTANDARD"

Ricardo, a 1st-grade student whose family speaks Portuguese at home, was referred to a special education team because of concerns about his reading progress. Both his reading intervention teacher and general education teacher provided several copies of his benchmark assessments as evidence of a possible language disorder or learning disability. Ricardo made miscues such as substituting the word *red* for *head*. He added numerous vowel sounds to the end of his words. The teachers also brought up a concern about Ricardo's hearing acuity because he seemed to nasalize his vowels and to read so loudly. Despite his teachers' deep concerns, Ricardo had made some progress over his first 2 years of school and tested in reading only a level or two below his peers.

Maya, a 3rd-grader, used American Sign Language (ASL) as her home language. As it turned out, Maya had normal hearing but had used ASL at home since she was a baby because her mother, stepfather, father, and several close family friends were all deaf. After listening to a story about Clifford the Big Red Dog (Bridwell, 1963) wishing to go to school with Emily Elizabeth, Maya wrote with great enthusiasm in her journal about the book: *Clifford bib (did) exted (excited) new shcol (school) Emily Elizabeth Yes!* Maya had already been identified as a student with learning disabilities, but her teacher wanted her to have more help with written expression in the special education resource room.

Jacob, who was Black and also a 1st-grader, was referred for special education evaluation. Because beginning readers are encouraged to match words with their fingers while reading so that they pay close attention to features of print and learn common sight words, Jacob often got confused when he verbally omitted words and found himself with "leftover" words to read. For example, a book contained the pattern: "This is my lunch, said the elephant. Yum! Yum! This is my lunch, said the lion. Yum! Yum!"

and so forth (Blaxland, 1996). A beginning reader would normally pick up the pattern, check the picture to identify the animal, and read independently. However, Jacob was omitting the word *is* (and occasionally *this*) and reading, "*This my lunch, said the elephant. Yum! Yum!*" After several tries, Jacob noticed the initial letters in *my* and *lunch* and placed his finger accordingly, but he still skipped the word *is*. His teacher was concerned about Jacob's inability to accurately match words with one-to-one correspondence and wanted to make sure that Jacob got special education help early on.

Nathan was identified as having a speech and language disorder because of stuttering and difficulties with word retrieval during his preschool years. Yet, as a 2nd-grade student, Nathan was still reading pattern books and attempting to use pictures as cues for words. Nathan had the most vexing time with retrieving vocabulary words, even when he was looking at pictures. He often complained, "I know what it is," or "I just can't say it," or "It won't come out!" Sometimes he would get mixed-up and say *kangaroo* instead of *grasshopper* or *zebra* instead of *giraffe*. Other times he would describe the word, such as *bam bam* for *thunder*. Nathan was constantly and automatically corrected by the adults around him and given word retrieval and speech fluency exercises during his speech and language therapy sessions. Even so, his teacher was concerned about his capabilities in reading and requested a referral for an additional eligibility as a student with learning disabilities.

Even though Ricardo, Maya, Jacob, and Nathan have had vastly different language and literacy experiences in their young lives, all four were learning how their spoken language knowledge and abilities transfer or do not transfer to written English. All four were attempting to make sense of what they read and wrote. And all four deserved full membership in a culturally, linguistically, and academically responsive general education classroom.

MISUNDERSTANDING LANGUAGE TRANSFER FROM NATIVE LANGUAGES AND "NONSTANDARD" FORMS OF SPEECH AND ENGLISH

Many students who are English language learners, who speak a variation of English, or have speech and language disorders like Ricardo, Maya, Jacob, and Nathan, start out their young lives using forms of spoken language that are different from the so-called "standard" written English found in most children's books and textbooks. Linguistic differences are often reflected in their written pieces, as was the case with Maya. Since the day they were born, Ricardo and Maya both encountered languages other than English in their respective homes and communities. They had little exposure to English until they arrived to kindergarten. Jacob started out his life using African American English (AAE), also referred to as African American Vernacular English, Black English, Black Vernacular English, or Ebonics—whose use, despite the terminology, is not always limited to people of African descent. Maya, who used ASL with her parents and family friends, also happened to converse in AAE with a few of her hearing family members and friends. In my experience, I have found that many students, like Nathan, who have speech and language disorders experience similar educational impacts on their English literacy learning as students who speak using either a native language other than English or a variation of English.

Although I have chosen to discuss characteristics of speech and language disorders in this chapter, I am not implying that those who are English language learners or those who speak another variation of English actually have a speech or language disability. Rather, these students' challenges with literacy stem from learning to reconcile print words with the spoken language that that they were accustomed to hearing and speaking at home and in their communities. However, Ricardo and Jacob were being referred for special education evaluation, Maya was already in special education, and Nathan indeed had a speech and language disorder, all because the students' attempts at reconciling print words with their spoken words were taken from a deficit viewpoint by their teachers. Their teachers thought that they would need or need *more* special education, and no one recognized that they were simply exploring, in a positive manner, the disconnect between print words and their speech.

The view of these students as having reading and writing deficits intersects with an outdated concept that oral language is a foundation of literacy. Oral language as a foundation of later reading and writing is a considerably early, and now outdated, research construction of how children learn to read and write. Later research has shown that children acquire written language alongside oral language and that the two are intertwined and interrelated throughout both processes of development (Sulzby, 1996). Oral language is just a foundation, such as the base of a four-tiered wedding cake. Most infants start out by hearing their mothers and fathers talk. This fosters receptive language, representing the base of the cake. Soon they begin to babble and talk themselves, developing their expressive language, which is represented by the second layer of the cake. The third layer of the cake represents learning to read, and the top fourth layer is learning to write. As children progress into the realm of print, receptive and expressive language areas are simultaneously enriched. Children learn more words and concepts

through reading and during discussions surrounding print. When they learn
to write, they think about structuring language for the purpose of conveying
meaning. *All* the layers together make a cake.

Being deaf myself, I often have to explain how I learned to read as a
young child. I clarify that a slice or two taken from the oral language base
does not collapse the whole cake. I learned to speak better *after* I had learned
to read. Likewise, a slice taken from the oral language base shouldn't collapse the whole cake for Ricardo making verbal "miscues" because of his
Portuguese accent, Maya writing in her journal using syntax from her ASL,
and Jacob getting confused when matching words. Even so, all three can
learn to read in English by taking an intertwined and interrelated, and positive, approach between their spoken languages and written English—making concrete distinctions and connections between language and literacy—in
a well-grounded and meaningful curriculum designed for all students. Even
Nathan can learn to use print as a resource to accommodate his stuttering
and word-retrieval disorders. In a bidirectional approach, oral language can
influence the learning of written language just as written language can shape
the understanding of oral language.

Urban, suburban, and rural schools all exhibit a surprising breadth of
linguistic diversity among students. Unfortunately, only 7% of 4th-grade
students and 3% of 8th-grade students who are English language learners (ELL) performed at or above the *Proficient* level in reading in 2013
(National Center for Education Statistics, 2013). Many educators are well
aware of the Black–White achievement gap in reading (Barton and Coley,
2010). Results from a study that classified 604 participants as poor or good
readers on the basis of reading performance in 2nd grade indicated that over
70% of poor readers had a history of language deficits, such as phonological processing and oral language, in kindergarten (Catts, Fey, Zhang, &
Tomblin, 1999). Unfortunately, invoking a deficit viewpoint to explain students' difficulties in interpreting spoken language that is mismatched with
the print they find in texts and books limits their opportunities for learning
to read and write throughout their educational careers. To put it briefly,
just because someone speaks differently for *any* reason does not mean that
person cannot learn to read proficiently or write effectively.

A Heterogeneous and Complex Population

The purpose of education in the United States is to ensure that students from
any walk of life can succeed in their educational and later economic pursuits.
Surely, Ricardo, Maya, Jacob, and even Nathan, should learn to read and write
in mainstream forms of English as their ticket to opportunities. However, given

the grim achievement data, many students from diverse linguistic backgrounds are taught in "disabling contexts," with too few opportunities to receive appropriate instruction matched to their needs and too few opportunities to develop their oral language and literacy skills (Klingner, 2014).

To exacerbate the problem further, few experimental studies have examined the effectiveness of complex innovations aimed at improving the literacy performance of English language learners (Shanahan & Beck, 2006). Teaching students like Ricardo in linguistically diverse schools is a controversial topic that has led to political debate, court decisions, and federal and state mandates.

Students with a first language other than English are classified as English language learners (ELLs). Ricardo, as an ELL, is part of a fast-growing segment of our country's school population. By the 2011–2012 school year, approximately 9.1% of public school students in the United States were participating in programs for ELLs. Some states are now reporting percentages as high as 15% to 20% (National Center for Education Statistics, 2014c). Yet, ELLs are also a highly heterogeneous and complex group; each individual has his or her own multiple language and literacy background and experiences. As with the reading wars, there are problems with mandating broad-sweeping methods or programs, minimal professional development for educators, and lack of provision for authentic and engaged reading experiences for students classified as ELLs, and all of these factors contribute to opportunity gaps. "By focusing on those students who are not proficient in English, we risk losing sight of the potential of the millions of bilingual and multilingual children in this country who can become national resources in building a peaceful coexistence within a global society and helping the United States remain economically viable in an increasingly multilingual world" (Garcia, Kleifgen, & Falchi, 2008, p. 11). Significant achievement gaps occur when language differences are viewed as a deficit or learning disability as opposed to embracing the concept that most students can and do become literate in multiple languages and language variations.

Students from diverse racial, ethnic, and linguistic backgrounds are educated primarily by White teachers (National Center for Education Statistics, 2014b). However, the reality is that every single speaker, regardless of languages, has an accent. Judgment about which accents are deemed socially acceptable or unacceptable are rooted in and supported by divisions within historical, social, and political contexts (American Association for Applied Linguistics, 2011). Dogma among schools that regard speech and/or language as "correct" or "standard" versus "incorrect" or "nonstandard" is likely to marginalize students and diminish their potential for accepting, embracing, and even learning a wider range of languages and literacies.

Types of Linguistic Difference

Not commonly part of English language learner programs for students in schools, American Sign Language (ASL) is indeed considered by linguists a rich, complex, and valid language with its own rules of grammar and syntax. Like all languages, ASL even has regional dialects and is a living language that grows and changes over time (National Association of the Deaf, 2014). Viewing ASL as a simple set of baby signs, crude gesturing, or mime is a form of judgment rooted within historical, social, and political contexts. Though she was not deaf, Maya made transfers from her home languages to her written pieces in school. Quite often, ASL has both a finger-spelled (representing the alphabet letter by letter) sign and a sign for the same concept (Valli & Lucas, 2000). However, both ASL and her other language, AAE, which have syntactical differences compared with written English, appeared in Maya's attempts to write sentences. Maya was, in essence, ordering and writing her words down in the way she knew how. Because her knowledge of her home languages was overlooked and seen as deficits in her writing, she was referred for additional special education services.

Definitions of linguistic diversity in schools cannot just consider the number of languages, such as Arabic, Cantonese, Russian or even ASL, spoken by the students and their families, but must also include variations of the English languages. Ribbing aside about Boston or Brooklyn accents, the Southern drawl, or the Yooper dialect, pronunciations, syntax, and vocabulary vary geographically and socioculturally, and even change over time. Equally controversial is asserting the legitimacy of variation as a *difference*, and not as English filled with mistakes, such as the presence of African American English and how it should be approached. In 1979, the court in the case of *Martin Luther King Junior Elementary School Children v. Ann Arbor School District* (also referred as the *Ann Arbor Decision*) ordered the school district to help teachers identify and take into account the students who spoke Black English in the educational process of teaching them to read in standard English (*Martin Luther King Junior Elementary School Children v. Ann Arbor School District*, 1979). Thus, the *Ann Arbor Decision* "laid the basis for instituting a language policy for the Black community that would have had far-reaching implications for other communities. Unfortunately, that goal was not realized" (Smitherman, 2002, p. 167). We find that many students like Jacob, reading aloud in his own language variation, are still at risk for referral to special education or another separate reading intervention program. The Black–White achievement gap continues to be a prevalent and concerning issue today.

Not only are there students who speak another language or a variation of English, but 21% of students in special education, including Nathan, are identified as having a speech and language impairment (National Center for Education Statistics, 2014a). Even though there may be a neurological basis for speech and language disorders, their speech can also be heard as a language variation instead of a disability. Nathan was indeed learning to read. He knew the words but could not always say them verbally. Eventually, as he got older, he was able to use sources of print, particularly as he became proficient at decoding, to support his spoken language.

Accounting for Language Variation when Teaching Literacy

Although it is valuable for all students to use forms of languages as appropriate for certain situations (such as at home, in school, or on the job) and it is important for speech and language to be at least comprehensible in any situation, it is imperative for educators to distinguish between speech production and comprehension. Most of us, as students and adults, can *understand* many forms of language, but are not competently able to *use* some languages ourselves (Stubbs, 2002, p. 77). Even though Ricardo made "miscues" in the form of his Portuguese accent, Maya attempted to write in ASL, Jacob omitted words that were not commonly used in his language variation, and Nathan struggled to retrieve words, all of the students were able to comprehend the content. They all used their own point of reference from their own language capabilities to maintain meaning in a positive and purposeful manner. Therefore, frequently correcting students only served to prevent them from using language and, later, literacy in an emotionally safe manner. Furthermore, correction outside of confidential therapy and practice sessions places a social judgment on what might be considered proper English instead of actively listening to the content of the message itself. Correcting speech and language in a public way only contributes to students' feelings of demoralization about their membership in the classroom and about their learning. The bottom line is that Ricardo, Maya, Jacob, and Nathan, along with many other students from culturally and linguistically diverse schools, desire to be heard for what they have to say.

In the same vein, noticing, scoring, or correcting while students are reading aloud on an exacting word-by-word, or even letter-by-letter, basis is unproductive in supporting linguistically diverse students' reading. Typically, students are assessed and monitored on their ability to orally read and answer a set of comprehension questions with the goal of selecting appropriately leveled materials for reading instruction. However, "basing the match on a student's oral reading performance is problematic because such an assessment tells little about the student's comprehension" (Fisher, Frey, & Lapp, 2012, p. 6). Expecting students to read aloud in an exacting manner hinders fluency and comprehension. And the vicious downward cycle continues when students are placed into a lower reading group based on their oral performance than would be appropriate if they were judged on their comprehension. Reading material below their interest levels in turn contributes to a lack of motivation and engagement. It doesn't take long for students to develop a deep-seated narrative that tells them they are unable to read, and they may even refuse to read altogether.

Requiring the rate of oral accuracy to be set at 95% or higher for benchmarking, leveling, or grouping purposes persists in most classrooms despite the lack of evidence that it is effective (Fisher, Frey, & Lapp, 2012). Maintaining the current practice of making referrals based on low accuracy rates places the problem within the individual student in a pathological manner. It is particularly unjust for students from linguistically diverse backgrounds because proficient and fluent readers make adjustments in their own language as they read for meaning and comprehension. When they are identified as *low-achieving*, students are more likely to be asked to read aloud, to have their attention focused on word recognition rather than comprehension, to spend more time working alone on low-level worksheets than on reading authentic texts, and to experience more fragmentation in their instructional activities (Walmsley & Allington, 1995). Instead, we need to explore the capabilities and experiences of young bilingual students as competent and dynamic language users and learners (Gort & Bauer, 2012). This holds true for students who have speech and language disorders, too. By focusing too closely on students' use of accents, syntax, and even vocabulary when obtaining oral accuracy rates, we set in motion the potential for an achievement gap throughout their entire educational career.

DISTINGUISHING ACHIEVEMENT GAPS VERSUS OPPORTUNITY GAPS

Ricardo, Jacob, Maya, and Nathan, for far-ranging reasons, spoke home languages that differed from the language found in most children's books and textbooks. All four, who were in the process of being referred for or were already situated in special education, were viewed as having deficits. It is common for Ricardo and other students learning English to apply knowledge from their first language to a second language. This is termed *language transfer* (or *L1 interference or linguistic interference*). In comparing the features of Portuguese and typical language transfers to English language learning (Shepard, 2001), the "errors" that Ricardo was making were relevant to his native language, and not a result of any learning disability. For example, the Portuguese language does not contain the phoneme /r/, so Ricardo pronounced the word *red* as *head*. There are few final consonants in Portuguese words, which explained why Ricardo added numerous vowel sounds to the end of his English words. There was concern about Ricardo's hearing acuity because he seemed to read so loudly, but the Portuguese language has a strong syllable stress and tends to be spoken with a lower pitch and higher volume. Maya, on the other hand, had not yet realized that there was no written form of ASL, but she placed some grammatical features of ASL in her attempts to write sentences. Jacob, using a variation of English, skipped the word *is* while reading a pattern book. This was not an indication of a learning disability; Jacob was merely reading for meaning and attempting to make sense of the interaction between his spoken language and the text. Nathan, who did have a speech and language disorder, was also reading for meaning, but learning to read would help improve his spoken language ability. Seeing letters, particularly initial letter-sounds, helped Nathan call up the correct vocabulary words. But because a deficit viewpoint was taken, Nathan was given isolated word retrieval and speech exercises at the cost of authentic opportunities to learn to read in either his general classroom or in special education.

The Achievement Gap	The Opportunity Gap
Achievement gaps occur through noticing, scoring, or correcting while students are reading aloud on an exacting word-by-word, or even letter-by-letter, basis. When we identify students as *low-achieving*, despite the fact that all proficient and fluent readers make adjustments in their own language as they read for meaning and comprehension, we set in motion their narrative as unable or unwilling to learn to read and write in multiple languages.	The gap that students who were identified as having reading deficits faced was not a direct result of their languages, language variations, or speech and language disorders but rather was because of few or a lack of opportunities for bridging their spoken languages with the literacy found in children's books and textbooks. Opportunity gaps are created by a lack of literacy instruction that is individualized, connected, meaningful, and multilingual.

Because Ricardo, Maya, Jacob, and Nathan did not receive opportunities for concrete instruction that distinguished and/or bridged their spoken languages with the language of print, the result was underachievement mistakenly interpreted as a learning disability in each of them. Quite often, students who are thought to have a learning disability do not, in fact, have one; rather, they are simply drawing on the patterns of their home language as they learn to read and write English. All of these students were at-risk of being underserved in an education system that continues to perpetuate inequity issues through the dogma that there is a "correct" or "standard" form of English, through a disregard of the linguistic characteristics that children start out their young lives with, or through ignorance of languages and their variations.

Spoken language is acquired naturally by exposure within a child's environment, but reading and writing are learned consciously. Steven Pinker (1997) reminded us that Charles Darwin got it right: Language is a human instinct, but written language is not. According to Pinker, children are wired for sound, but print is an optional accessory that must be painstakingly bolted on. We were never born to read; human beings invented reading only a few thousand years ago (Wolf, 2007). A contributing factor to opportunity gaps comes from policymakers and educators who do not see language from a neutral viewpoint but instead define language as either "standard" or "nonstandard." Most consider it appropriate to teach and conduct school in "standard" English because it is the mainstay of educational and economic opportunity in our country. However, teachers carry a special responsibility to help distinguish and bridge linguistic differences so that written English is accessible to all students. "By failing to acknowledge the legitimacy of Ebonics and other varieties of English, restrictive proposals place the burden for bridging linguistic differences between the child and the school squarely on the child" (Wiley, 2005, p. 12). It is an awful lot to expect of a 5- to 8-year-old child, who arrives with only the language of his or her home and community and is trying to learn to read. When there is a mismatch between spoken and written languages because of second-language learning, accents, dialects, speech and language disorders, and so forth, there is a risk for opportunity gaps to arise in reading and writing instruction—not because of the spoken language itself, but more so because of a lack of instructional support (the bolts) for making meaningful connection between the home language and written English.

Opportunity gaps occur when educators *intentionally* overlook the extent of linguistic diversity that students bring to their classrooms or schools. Although dogma about "standard English," if folded into educational policy and curriculum, does contribute to opportunity gaps in reading instruction, a *disregard* of linguistic characteristics, when assessing or teaching reading, is equally damaging. Being "neutral" involves educators viewing all their students as equals and subjecting them to the same curriculum and assessments, no matter what their linguistic background might be. By ignoring language variations, educators may intend to evaluate reading progress and merit against curriculum standards and thereby maintain high expectations for all. However, failure to acknowledge the interrelationships between languages and text prevents some students from building metalinguistic awareness—a conscious awareness on the part of the language user of language as an object in itself (Harris & Hodges, 1995). Students may feel lost and confused. Maya and Jacob both were victims of this viewpoint. Because Maya had multiple languages—ASL, AAE, and written English—to juggle without support, she complained that she felt stupid for being wrong all the time. Jacob was confused when matching words with one-to-one correspondence while reading as he omitted words even though his own sentences sounded right to him. Students benefit from concrete instruction, using authentic and natural language books, acknowledging the many different ways people speak and that this speech does not always exactly match the words in books. Most important, students need to hear that they can still learn to read and write.

Lacking knowledge about a student's language, English language variation, or speech and language disorder and wrongly interpreting language difference as a reading disability may cause teachers to inadvertently contribute to opportunity gaps. Of course, teachers cannot be expected to have expertise on every language or language variation they come across. However, because they position students for success or failure by influencing students' self-perceptions as readers, teachers can examine their attitudes, beliefs, and instructional practices related to culture and language (Risko & Walker-Dalhouse, 2012). Withholding the judgment that something might be wrong with the students, teachers can dig deeper by collaborating on assessment information or observations of linguistically diverse students with colleagues or consult with speech and language pathologists, expert linguists, or translators. Ricardo found himself on the school's referral team because of his teachers' ignorance about his Portuguese language. When his teachers came to understand the valid transfers he was making as he was reading in written English, they were able to see him as a more capable reader than they originally thought. By accepting his accents and nasalization, his teachers realized that Ricardo's miscues, which did not change meaning, were not true errors and did not mark them as such when doing reading assessments. That way, he could keep making progress and increase his exposure to the world of books closer to grade (and interest) level. When there is collaborative acknowledgment, connection, and bridging of various languages in diverse classrooms, student achievement in reading will be higher than otherwise expected.

ACKNOWLEDGING LANGUAGE VARIATION IN CHANGING THE TRAJECTORIES OF CHILDREN LEARNING ENGLISH IN PRINT

Running records is a method of taking notes while observing a student reading aloud a short passage and later analyzing both the accuracy and types of errors made in order to determine what strategies a student may or may not be using. Frequent and informal use of running records can serve as an excellent source for inquiry about students' diverse language and literacy development (Houk, 2005). Note, though, that noticing, scoring, or correcting while students are reading aloud on an exacting word-by-word, or even letter-by-letter, basis is unproductive in supporting linguistically diverse students in learning to read. Running records is for the teacher's own use in informing instruction and support to help students make distinctions and connections from their home languages to written English. It shouldn't be simply scored and reported for accountability purposes, but instead should be used only as a meaningful resource for planning small-group or individual reading lessons and literacy activities.

Although running records can reduce ignorance of linguistic characteristics among educators, there is an inherent danger of returning to and taking on the viewpoint that language is "standard" versus "nonstandard" and believing that students must be explicitly taught the difference in a judgmental manner. A judgmental viewpoint has the potential to create the message that students are not readers, even though they are fully capable of comprehending the content. There is a danger of disregarding linguistic characteristics, such as scoring all miscues even if the meaning was not changed, in order to maintain fairness and merit against curriculum standards among all students. When accuracy rates are used for the purpose of benchmarking or leveling and are taken with a deficit viewpoint, this can cause achievement gaps. The use of running records is only powerful when it is done with the purpose of observing, inquiring, and supporting students in literacy instruction.

Because of a disconnect between their various home or spoken languages and in written English, Ricardo, Maya, Jacob, and Nathan were seen as having deficits in their ability to learn to read or write. They were in the process of being referred or had already been placed in special education. If we were to change their trajectory in their educational career, we could begin by digging deeper into the linguistic patterns they brought to school. Teachers could recognize that their errors are a sign of progress and an indication that the students are feeling comfortable enough to take risks (Klingner, Almanza de Schonewise, Onis, & Barletta, 2008). Errors also reflect these students' attempts to make meaning based on their understandings of both their native and English languages. Ricardo, Maya, Jacob, and Nathan were learning to read and write; all had been motivated and disciplined students, and all were fully engaged in exploring the world of print in multiple languages and language variations, even (for Nathan) despite a speech and language disorder.

By making the distinction between language itself and the deeply entrenched attitudes and stereotypes most people hold about language, we can begin to remove moral censure (Stubbs, 2002) from our interpretation of students' processes of learning to read and write. There is evidence from classroom and community-based research that suggests biliteracy can be attained with deliberate support, continued encouragement, opportunity, and high-quality instruction in two languages in classroom settings and beyond (Gort & Bauer, 2012). Ricardo, Maya, Jacob, and Nathan, along with other students like them, needed to see their unique places as a positive place where multilingualism and multiliteracy is fully accepted, embraced, and encouraged. Emergent bilingual children are able to navigate two languages and use their developing knowledge of these languages to engage themselves and others in thinking about how their languages work (Bauer & Gort, 2012). There is no reason to view them as disabled or to limit their use of home languages and literacies to serve only as a bridge to reading and writing in English. Teachers may ask themselves the following questions as they move toward eliminating educational opportunity gaps for linguistically diverse students:

All Students Are Emerging as Multilingual and Multiliterate

What does your inner voice say about your students with a background in a variation of English or another language who are learning English? Listen to it carefully. How can you shift your focus from the skills and English competencies that students haven't yet learned to proactive and positive ways of understanding their unique backgrounds and resulting linguistic skills?

When teachers redefine the concept of "errors" in students' reading or writing to that of seeing that all students are in emotionally safe places in their different exploration of multiple languages and literacies, they are in a better position to develop a stronger sense of metalinguistic awareness among all students, and even adults, in their schools. They can allow students to read for meaning in any way that makes sense to them. They can avoid placing students into a lower reading group than appropriate or into a separate and fragmented reading program. They can work toward maintaining a sense of community, interest, motivation, and engagement. Most of all, they can develop a strong narrative that all students *can* learn to read and write, no matter the language diversity they bring to school.

All Kinds of Families, All Kinds of Languages, All Kinds of Literacies

Some families foster literacy in their home languages but expect schools to teach in English. How can you embrace the multiple forms and variations of languages and literacies that students and their families bring to school?

When teachers demonstrate full inclusion for a culturally, linguistically, and academically diverse group of students, they are in a better place for approaching and including families in their process of creating multilingual and multiliterate schools. Just as the deficit model undermines our work with students in the classrooms, it also poisons our work with families and communities (Houk, 2005). All families, no matter what language they choose to use at home, can contribute positively to their children's success in learning written English at school. Their positive contributions need to be recognized in the context of their economic, cultural, and linguistic backgrounds, rather than in the context of what we, in schools, consider a "correct" or "standard" form of English.

Beginning With What Is Known

In what ways can you start with and build upon what students already know about language and literacies?

Teachers who learn about and embrace multiple languages and literacies as variation instead of deficits become high-quality and effective teachers. They are astute in understanding literacy development for students whose language, language variation, or speech and language disorder is different from what is found in children's books and textbooks. They make an attempt to understand the vocabulary, phonological, syntactic, and pragmatic confusions that might stymie students' progress in reading and writing

(Helman, 2012), yet at the same time, view "errors" as progress toward being accomplished readers and writers.

Developing a Flexible and Responsive Curriculum

How can your classroom environment and curriculum routines be structured so that all students' home literacies are valued during literacy activities?

Despite the overwhelming evidence in support of the use of students' home languages in their school, emergent bilinguals are increasingly in classrooms where their home languages are disregarded (Garcia, Kleifgen, & Falchi, 2008). The reality is that even young students can continue to develop their home language, see how it transfers (or does not transfer) to the English found in print, and learn to gain meaning from written English.

In recognizing that language is both personal and complex (Helman, 2012), linguistically responsive teachers allow students and adults to be both teachers and learners of languages. Teachers can ask and carry on conversations with students about their attempts to read letters, words, and sentences in order to support their overlapping languages and especially in order to learn about the languages the students bring to school. There is no reason to limit inquiry as to whether a miscued word or phrase looks right, sounds right, or makes sense. After all, even though the words for Jacob in the pattern about lunch didn't match up, his reading did sound right and made sense to him. And just as well, Nathan can continue reading without having to stutter and struggle to verbally state the words *grasshopper*, *giraffe*, and *thunder*. Developing a rapport of linguistic understanding between students and their teachers makes for a strong and emotionally safe multilingual and multiliterate environment.

Taking Back Ownership and Leadership

Are your students taking part in a well-rounded, authentic multilingual and multiliteracy curriculum that values home languages and language variations during read-aloud time, shared reading, independent reading, guided reading, writing, and word work?

Even though multilingualism is commonplace in contemporary states, there are widespread ideological programs supporting monolingual policies (Tollefson, 2013). The tendency over the past decade has been for policymakers and the public more generally to support English-only programs and to move away from programs that use the child's home languages, despite abundant research evidence that this is the wrong emphasis (Garcia, Kleifgen, & Falchi, 2008). English immersion, a model that places English language learners into all-English classrooms with little or no additional support or instructional modification to develop language or content proficiency, is also referred to as a *submersion* or *sink-or-swim* model (Garcia, Kleifgen, & Falchi, 2008; Houk, 2005). Unfortunately, students like Ricardo, Maya, Jacob, and even Nathan have the potential to sink, and become disengaged, when there is an expectation that all specific (and fragmented and isolated) skills in English must be in place before they can truly be capable of reading or writing. However, when teachers honor both oral and written home languages in school, they validate the student's point of power in learning; thus, academic investment is most likely to occur (DelliCarpini, 2010). Students should have a choice of which language or dialect they use to complete activities (DelliCarpini, 2010) in that they have metalinguistic awareness and intention, become fully engaged, have power and control over their learning, become critical thinkers, and add to their already-sophisticated repertoire of their home languages.

Rethinking Book Fairs and Pajama Nights

Many literacy events such as parent-teacher conferences, book fairs, and pajama nights are often uncomfortable for families who do not feel that they understand or speak in English well enough to participate. How can you ensure that events are accessible to families who speak multiple languages and welcome diversity?

Schoolwide events such as parent-teacher conferences, book fairs, or pajama nights are most often planned and presented in English. General education teachers, along with their administrators, may want to rethink such events from the perspective of families and take steps to minimize the language barriers for them to participate. Making sure the entire building and school-wide programs and materials are universally designed to embrace multiple languages and literacies from the beginning goes a long way toward increasing participation among all families.

LANGUAGE, LANGUAGE, AND LANGUAGE

In recognizing and fully accepting that language and literacy in schools around our country is becoming increasingly diverse, a strong, positive and comprehensive multilingual and multiliteracy environment becomes necessary. All individuals—no matter what language, language variation, or speech and language disorder they bring to school—are fully capable of becoming strong readers and effective writers when provided with adequate and emotionally safe support to develop metalinguistic awareness and intention.

CHAPTER 5

You Can't Judge a Book by Its Cover

Wesley and Sam were both Black 5th-grade boys who were reading three grade levels below their classmates. Wesley had chronic ear infections as a preschooler, resulting in a mild hearing loss in one ear. Sam was a sensitive soul, prone to crying and tantrums, who found himself labeled emotionally impaired. Both ended up in special education during their 1st-grade years; however, by 5th grade, Wesley's ear infections had long since healed and Sam was no longer crying at school. Wesley happened upon a book, *The Whipping Boy* (Fleischman, 1986), and was immediately intrigued by the title. This book is about a commoner boy living in a king's castle who takes punishment in place of Prince Brat, whom it is illegal to spank. The special education teacher helped the boys read it despite the fact that the text was well above their reading level. Even though it was not directly stated and the illustrations didn't show it, Sam insisted that the Whipping Boy was Black. This led to many conversations among the three of them about the boys' experiences with self-perceived discrimination and why they seemed to find themselves in trouble at school a lot.

Dwayne was also Black, just beginning 5th grade, and no one really knew why he was not reading well. He had no risk factors such as poverty, low birth weight, or lead or mercury poisoning. He was in perfect health and physically fit. There were no behavioral concerns. He came from a stable home environment with two parents, several younger siblings, and an extended family, and his first language was a standard form of English. Dwayne was brought to a referral team because he was found to be two grade levels behind in reading. When Dwayne's reading test scores fell behind, he was automatically placed in a Title I–funded reading classroom that used an online reading intervention program for 90 minutes a day, although his teacher and the Title I teacher did not have a clear understanding of what his specific instructional needs were. Dwayne's reading classroom had always had a high rate of minority students (as compared with the rest of the school) over the years. However, like many other students, he had been attending this program for almost 2 years without making much progress. Thus, his teachers were concerned that he might have a learning disability.

A 2nd-grade teacher was concerned about a student, Lamar, who was also Black, spoke African American English, and was not making progress with reading. The principal called Lamar's father, a single dad, and arranged a meeting to discuss referring Lamar for special education. It became alarmingly clear that there had been no prior communication between Lamar's teacher and his father, who had no idea why he had been called to the meeting. However, Lamar's father knew that education was important and was willing to take valuable time off from his hourly job to meet with Lamar's teacher. After listening for a few minutes to the teacher's concerns, he angrily made it clear that he knew *about this Black special education thing going on.* He declared that he would have no more of these meetings and there was no way he would sign any papers for special education. He wrote down his cellphone number and uttered his final words: *You teach him. I discipline him. If he gives you trouble, you call me right away.* Then he walked right out of that conference room.

THE ROLE OF RACE IN SPECIAL EDUCATION REFERRALS

How right Lamar's father was. Because of the systemic structure in our schools, many students with Black or Brown skin, particularly boys, are placed on special education caseloads, some for dubious reasons. Wesley and Sam knew that reading was difficult for them and that was why they were getting extra help in the resource room, but they never saw themselves as having a disability or being in need of special education—they simply saw themselves as Black, from their cultural and linguistic viewpoint. In the conversations surrounding *The Whipping Boy* and their personal experiences, Wesley and Sam had never indicated a perception of the resource room being a place for people with disabilities. It is not clear whether Dwayne saw himself as Black, but the opportunity gap in his reading instruction occurred because of his placement, based on a simple test score, in a Title I classroom with reduced expectations. Although the school may not have intentionally placed him in the Title I classroom because of his race, statistics have shown in an array of data collection and research projects that Black, Hispanic, and American Indian/Alaska Native students overall are underperforming in reading achievement in comparison with their White peers (U.S. Department of Education, 2013), and these students are placed into remedial or special programs in disproportionate numbers (National Association of School Psychologists, 2007). Although poverty and wealth do have an impact on student achievement, without question, "statistically, however, even within the same economic strata, there is an achievement gap based on race" (Singleton & Linton, 2006, p. 29). A literacy gap was occurring even for Dwayne, who had no risk factors, came from a family having economic means and a stable home environment, and spoke a standard form of English.

Lamar's father, who was apparently aware of this trend, immediately detected his son's problems with reading as a "Black special education thing." Both Wesley and Sam, along with Lamar's father, were consciously and constantly aware of being Black in the schools. White people (being the majority of teachers), on the other hand, tend to think of racial identity as something other people have, not something that is salient for them (Tatum, 1997). As Glenn Singleton (2006) argues, schools are fundamentally not designed to educate students of color and educators continue to lack the capacity to affirm racial diversity.

Throughout the story of *The Whipping Boy*, Wesley, Sam, and their teacher (who was White) were in a safe place to affirm their races, which in turn had a positive impact on the boys' literacy growth. Culturally responsive teaching can be defined as "using the cultural knowledge, prior experience, frames of references, and performance styles of ethnically diverse students to make learning encounters more relevant to and effective for them" (Gay, 2010, p. 31). Both Wesley and Sam had a wealth of knowledge that was not transferred to the school environment because in general, schools have developed an unstated framework for what is considered acceptable, comfortable, and safe literacy. Even though the emotionally and historically charged topic of racial injustices may feel unsafe for many teachers to bring up in their classrooms, both Wesley and Sam clearly demonstrated their intellectual astuteness in responding to *The Whipping Boy*. Singleton encourages teachers to keep a spotlight on race when engaging in discussions among themselves about achievement gaps. It is a difficult conversation for teachers, one wrought with feelings of fear, defensiveness, resistance, denial, and even colorblindness. Yet, when a conversation about race drifts to issues of, say, poverty, language, family values, or even disabilities, it diverts the attention away from recognizing and exploring issues of race. Otherwise, race—as an important key to the issue of opportunity gaps in reading and writing instruction for all students—may be missing.

Race-Based Inequality in Schools

One of the most unrelenting social issues in the United States involves gaps, such as disparities in educational, economic, or political opportunities and achievement, among groups characterized by race, ethnicity, language, gender, sexual identity, economic status, or disability. There is little recognition, on the part of the dominant White culture as a system, of the historical and structural relationships shaping our climate of social inequity. Thus, initiatives, programs, and policies that attempt to respond to gaps are likely to fall short (Brown & Donnor, 2011). Even though the days of overt racial segregation, from slavery to Jim Crow laws, are gone, inequality, racism, and racial discrimination continue to be manifested in a subtle and covert manner. Because we have elected a president and have many corporate leaders and esteemed professionals in medicine, engineering, and the arts who have Black or Brown skin, there is an implicit belief that we no longer have racial inequity issues. Yet, unacceptable numbers of persons with Black or Brown skin continue to have minimal educational attainment and low levels of literacy, be in poor health, be underemployed, or even be incarcerated as compared with their White counterparts. And unacceptable numbers of students, like Wesley, Sam, Dwayne, and Lamar, underperform in literacy early in their educational careers.

Although the racial gap for *illiteracy*, which refers to the inability to read and write at all, has narrowed to an inconsequential rate since the 19th and early 20th centuries (National Assessment of Adult Literacy, 2013b), there continues to be a racial gap for so-called *functional literacy* skills of adults over the age of 16. The criteria for functional literacy varies by study and situation, but it can be broadly defined as having the level of reading and writing sufficient for adult responsibilities as citizens and in the workplace (Harris & Hodges, 1995). The National Center for Education Statistics (2013) defined literacy in three parameters: prose, document, and quantitative literacy. In the last nationally measured survey of adults aged 16 or older, the Black–White differences ranged from 44 to 59 points in the average scores of these three areas of literacy skills (National Assessment of Adult Literacy, 2013a).

Today, our technology-driven, diverse, and quickly changing global economy has raised the bar for functional literacy in education and the workplace, requiring proficiency with the tools of technology, creating, critiquing, analyzing, and evaluating multimedia texts, and collaboratively and cross-culturally solving problems (National Council of Teachers of English, 2009). Though Wesley, Sam, and Dwayne were reading below expectations, they were not considered "illiterate." However, they were described by their teachers as "unable to read" because they were offered so little opportunity to demonstrate their capabilities and growth otherwise. If the term *literacy* is expanded to include many types of literacies, such as academic literacy, media literacy, cultural literacy, workplace literacy, computer literacy, and so forth, then it further categorizes students by their competence—or incompetence—in the each of the types of literacy they confront. The binary classification of individuals as either literate or illiterate stigmatizes and labels individuals as being different from others, questions their moral worth and productivity as employees and viable citizens, and causes many ills in our society, such as unemployment, dependency on assistance, and even incarceration.

The Current Achievement Gap and Its Companion, Disproportionality

Familiar to educators is the particularly vexing issue surrounding the achievement gap and its companion, *disproportionality*. The achievement gap refers to the disparity seen on a variety of assessment methods, such as statewide testing or local benchmark assessments, between groups characterized by race, gender, ability, and economic status. According to a continuing and nationally representative measure of reading achievement over time, significant racial/ethnic gaps among groups of 4th- and 8th-graders have persisted in the area of reading since 1992 (National Assessment of Educational Progress, 2014). *Disproportionality* refers to the overrepresentation of students with Black or Brown skin eligible for special education, raising the possibility that a percentage of them may not truly be disabled. Wesley, Sam, Dwayne, and Lamar were part of, or quickly becoming a part of, this disproportionality at each of their schools. The Committee on Minority Representation in Special Education from the National Research Council determined that in the "low-incidence categories (deaf, blind, or orthopedic impairment, etc.) in which the problem is observable outside the school context and is typically diagnosed by medical professionals, no marked disproportion exists. The higher representation of minority students occurs in the high-incidence categories of mild mental retardation (MMR), emotional disturbance (ED), and to a lesser extent learning disabilities (LD), categories in which the problem is often identified first in the school context and the disability diagnosis is typically given without confirmation of an organic cause" (Donovan & Cross, 2002, p. 1). Although disproportionality is a complicated and multifaceted issue that can be attributed to a variety of factors such as poverty, assessment bias, cultural difference, and compliance, minority status appears to be a contributing factor for special education eligibility (Zhang, Katsiyannis, Ju, & Roberts, 2014). No matter its cause, data showing achievement gaps and disproportionality in special education remain concerning despite years of debate, policies, and programs.

The Discipline Gap

Interwoven with the issue of the achievement gap and disproportionality is the *discipline gap*. The discipline gap concerns itself with the racially disproportionate numbers of students who are subjected to harsh exclusionary school disciplinary practices—namely, suspensions and expulsions. The U.S. Department of Education's Office for Civil Rights noted in a press release that African American students, particularly males, face harsher discipline and are far more likely to be suspended or expelled from school than their peers (Office of Civil Rights, 2012). Wesley and Sam were fully aware of this and pointed it out during their numerous discussions of *The Whipping Boy*. Some school administrators and superintendents are starting to envision closing the discipline gap as a possible step toward eliminating their district's achievement gap. Not only do exclusionary disciplinary practices cause students to miss valuable instructional time in school, but they also cause students like Wesley and Sam to see themselves as marginalized as both students and readers.

All three sets of inequity issues—binary classifications of students as literate versus illiterate, achievement gaps and disproportionality, and discipline gaps—impact students with Black or Brown skin nationwide, not only in high-poverty urban areas but also in rural and even affluent suburban areas. Even smaller cities, those that contain a major research university with a history of high academic achievement, and areas with plentiful social resources are not immune. Attempts to be colorblind often obscure the importance of race, causing opportunity gaps to be blamed on poverty, language, family values, or even disabilities. This futile "colorblindness" lends itself to a deficit viewpoint that blames individuals or their families for the lack of reading proficiency without requiring schools to acknowledge the lack of equitable opportunities for individuals or families. This is particularly true for males with Black or Brown skin like Wesley, Sam, Dwayne, and Lamar. Unfortunately, "articulations and responses to the Black male crisis circuitously perpetuate a racialized understanding of this population" (Brown & Donnor, 2011, p. 18). Both Scott (1997) and Noguera (2008) noted that decades of discourse and policy portrayed Black males as "culturally and psychologically damaged" or as "troubled" for a list of reasons such as having an "absent father," apathy and powerlessness, being too streetwise, having a tendency toward misbehavior and violence, being too focused on sports, and even illiteracy, all of which affirm the population's pathology. Therefore, initiatives and programs developed to address the needs of this population, which are often based on providing role models and mentors, tackling apathy, developing zero-tolerance disciplinary methods, or offering literacy classes, are based on this deficit viewpoint. It may be counterproductive because their goals work toward helping students adopt the behavioral, cultural, and linguistic values of the dominant population before they can have full access to literacy instruction and an education. As a result of this viewpoint, initiatives continue to fail to hold schools designed by a dominant culture responsible for inequities in education. Framing race in a pathological manner, even unintentionally, pinpoints the unequal and unjust arrangements of power and privilege in our schools as a microcosm of our larger society.

DISTINGUISHING ACHIEVEMENT GAPS VERSUS OPPORTUNITY GAPS

All three 5th-graders—Wesley, Sam, and Dwayne—were reading well below their grade levels, and all were Black. All three were removed from their classrooms for a significant portion of their school day because of academic underperformance. Lamar, also Black but only in 2nd grade, would already have been well on his way to identification for special education if it weren't for his father. All of the boys were seen as part of the achievement gap on multiple levels: by their teachers, by their school administrators, and by education policy statisticians who document gaps. Unfortunately, all were at-risk of being underserved in an education system that continues to perpetuate inequity issues by disproportionately placing students with different cultural and linguistic backgrounds in special education (or other separate programs) or subjecting them to harsh exclusionary school disciplinary practices. Viewing these students through the lens of an achievement gap ignores the fact that they may have had little opportunity to learn to read and write, all the while maintaining their sense of cultural and linguistic identity.

The Achievement Gap	The Opportunity Gap
Achievement gaps occur when historic and current inequity issues impacting students, like Wesley, Sam, and Dwayne, with Black or Brown skin are diverted to issues of disabilities, poverty, language, or even family values. It can also occur when students with Black or Brown skin are disproportionately placed in special education (or other separate programs) or subjected to harsh exclusionary school disciplinary practices.	Schools try to provide "opportunities" in the form of intervention or special education services. On the contrary, this brings lowered expectations on the part of general education teachers, parents, peers, and even students themselves. It conveys the message that these students do not belong in general education because they need special help. Thus, special education (or other separate programs) becomes a covert form of segregation.

The school system viewed Wesley, Sam, Dwayne, and Lamar through their supposed shortcomings, deeming their background or circumstances somehow responsible for their underachievement, rather than acknowledging the inadequacy of the educational system to teach them effectively. Exacerbating the situation for traditionally underperforming groups of students, the very culture of technology-driven, diverse, and quickly changing global economy continues to define and redefine literacy versus illiteracy without ensuring true educational opportunities for all students. "The assumptions held toward Black males that allow them to be regarded largely as a problem, pathologize their needs, and deny them the opportunity to learn must be thoroughly discussed, debated, and challenged" (Noguera, 2008, p. xxi). When their flaws are framed as a person-centered problem, the vicious cycle of stigmatization and branding continues for this population.

"Special Help" as a Covert Form of Racial Segregation

As with Wesley, Sam, Dwayne, and Lamar, the majority of students in special and gifted education are referred by general education teachers (Donovan & Cross, 2002; MacMillan & Siperstein, 2002; Redfield & Kraft, 2012). However, "if a teacher is biased in evaluating student performance and behavior, current procedures provide ample room for those biases to be reflected in referrals" (Donovan & Cross, 2002, p. 5). The fact that the American teaching force is predominantly White strengthens the likelihood of implicit bias in the referral process (Redfield & Kraft, 2012). Even teachers with good intentions who would not consider themselves racially biased can nevertheless contribute to disparity in special education by referring students to special education, citing real concern about a problem with retaining curriculum material, struggles with reading, or a specific situation at home. Usually, teachers have reached a point of helplessness by the time they refer a student and feel strongly that the student needs *special* help, especially in reading. "The referral is a signal that the teacher has reached the limits of his or her tolerance of individual differences, is no longer optimistic about his or her capacity to deal effectively with a particular student in the context of the larger group, and no longer perceives that the student is teachable by him- or herself" (Zigmond, 1993, pp. 262–263). Thus, a teacher's reasonable response is to seek expert help. Unfortunately, in seeking special help for a particular student, the teacher inadvertently shifts the responsibility to the student rather than the system that is failing to provide that student with culturally and linguistically responsive instruction.

Special help can take any form of special or alternative education such as special education, Title I services, English as Second Language (ESL) classes, reading intervention, computer programs, or other support programs. Often, the allocation of special help is based on test scores rather than an individual evaluation of where particular students are in their exploration of literacy. When the particular literacy skills and challenges of each student are not taken into account, this "special help" becomes a disadvantage, creating a vicious cycle of underachievement throughout an entire educational career. Dwayne fell into this trap when he was placed into a Title I classroom for a significant portion of his mornings by educators who did not have a clear understanding of his literacy growth. Labeling a student as struggling, learning disabled, dyslexic, or otherwise as having a disorder has serious implications, because *more help is not always better or even effective.* Current classification schemes, including referral procedures, testing, and remedial approaches, do not discriminate adequately among the various manifestations of learning processes. A student is likely to be matched to a program or approach as much by chance or by availability of funding as by accurate and appropriate diagnosis followed up with appropriate remediation (Walmsley & Allington, 1995). Students with all kinds of eligibilities are placed on different caseloads, causing them to spend inordinate amounts of time being pulled out or aside for instructional support services or therapy, thereby missing out on time in the mainstream classroom. Sam, who was identified as emotionally impaired, hardly ever spent time in his general education classrooms, and he missed instruction in other subject areas and fell further behind. Furthermore, attempts to remove students from special education caseloads or reduce their service times are often met with anxiety and resistance as opposed to being welcomed as good news. If this vicious cycle sounds like segregation, that's because it *is.*

Poverty, poor nutrition, low birth weight, exposure to lead or mercury, amount of television watching, the level of parental involvement, and other factors have been identified as correlates to achievement gaps. "The unavoidable conclusion is that if we are to close the gaps in achievement, we must first close the gaps in these life experiences and conditions" (Barton & Coley, 2009, p. 3). The problems of society, of course, are too overwhelming for a school system to solve. On the other hand, schools continue to perpetuate these social problems by unwittingly blurring *ableism* (as discussed in Chapter 3) with *racism* within its walls. Beginning when students are young, the playing field in education is not level, even though it is intended to prepare our future generations for college and the workforce. B. A. Ferri and D. J. Connor (2005) argue that overt racial segregation has given way to more covert forms of racial segregation, such as placement in special education. They argue that *disability,* instead of race, has become a socially accepted, even normalized, category of marginalization for students of color.

Although school factors including rigor of the curriculum, teacher preparation, teacher experience and turnover, and class size do contribute to achievement gaps (Barton & Coley, 2009), most concerning is the fact that students who fall outside the system's definition of "normal" must receive consent by teachers in order to belong to and learn in general education classrooms because of the social construction of what is considered "normal." Desegregation, integration, regular education initiatives, mainstreaming, and inclusion are some of the many names that have been attached to the idea of students being "allowed" to enter the school community (Jones, White, Fauske, & Carr, 2011). It becomes necessary to stop helplessly looking at what is *wrong* with some of our students and the circumstances they bring to school and move toward ensuring rich opportunities for all in our school systems.

Re-Envisioning Response-to-Intervention to Provide Targeted Help

Response-to-Intervention (RTI), one of many national and local attempts to narrow achievement gaps and reduce disproportionality, is intended to reduce the number of misdiagnoses for special education, particularly for students who were not taught adequately in the first place. Lamar's father knew his son's teachers should have communicated with him at the first sign of Lamar's lack of reading progress. Lamar should have been given adequate instruction in reading by a teacher who was mindful of his cultural and linguistic background. Beginning with an established baseline and appropriate goals, this teacher should have assessed Lamar's progress regularly to monitor whether the intervention was working for him or not. As a practical means to implement RTI, many schools nationwide utilize a multitiered model that is often illustrated in a triangle or flow chart (Fuchs & Fuchs, 2009). Most literacy learning needs are met through Tier 1, the general education classroom. Students who are found to be "at-risk" through schoolwide screening or benchmark monitoring may be provided with more intense, small-group intervention in Tier 2. Finally, those who show insufficient progress are considered for special education in Tier 3. Inherent in this multitiered design is a continuation of the segregation of some students with new, and perhaps seemly more politically correct, terminology. Instead of being labeled as *Title I, English Language Learner (ELL)* or *special education*, these groups are gently designated *Tier 2* or *Tier 3*. During the second year of transitioning into RTI at Dwayne's school, in which 28% of students were Black or biracial, it was discovered that out of the 19% of students receiving intervention, 47% were Black or biracial students. Unfortunately, this pattern of racial disproportionality was similar to what was originally found in special education in that students were placed in a separate and fragmented literacy program only under a new guise of RTI.

The editors of the *Reading Research Quarterly* (International Reading Association, 2006), in discussing current issues in special education and reading instruction, stated that "while reading is the most common point of contact between literacy and special education researchers, it has not been unusual that these two research communities view learning to read much differently" (p. 92). Alas, history appears to be repeating itself; there is now a cohort within each tier that discusses and chooses which "scientifically based intervention," including programs of a commercial nature, will be implemented in the tier for which they are responsible.

Although RTI attempts to serve as a preventative measure for later underachievement and placement in special education, the reauthorized Individuals with Disabilities Act (IDEA) also states that RTI and progress monitoring can be part of the *evaluative* process for determination of a disability. Even so, there are teachers who consider RTI simply another prolonged step toward special education as opposed to an early intervention and preventative policy. The current multitier model of RTI is often illustrated as a triangle, with the general education population representing the base and special education population the apex. Instead, my suggestion is to envision the multitier model as three or more pyramids as *insets* of itself, not unlike Russian nested dolls. Rather than transitioning up a triangle, or following some kind of protocol or flow chart, in trial-and-error fashion, we should envision getting to the *inside* of what is really going on with a student learning to read. The question then becomes: How can we support students in their literacy growth without unnecessarily and arbitrarily passing the problem on to another jurisdiction?

Ableism, when grouped with ignorance of diverse languages, classism, and racism, causes a disadvantageous opportunity gap for students in schools. Most often, some students are seen as *unable* or *unwilling* to make progress in reading or to access the curriculum. They are identified for what they *cannot* do, and somehow the responsibility falls on the student's family to *overcome* their situation, cultural differences, or priorities in order for their students to fully participate in and benefit from the education offered in schools. From an ableist (or deficit) viewpoint, schools try to provide "opportunities" in the form of intervention or special education services. However, doing this actually brings lowered expectations on the part of general education teachers, parents, peers, and even the students themselves. It conveys the message that these students do not belong in general education programs. Through the use of screening scores and one-size-fits-all reading programs, even students who are not in special education may be placed in one or more intervention programs without careful thought or communication among educators. "When a child cannot learn without the additional supports, *and* when the supports improve outcomes for the child, that trade-off may well be worth making. But because there is a trade-off, both the need and benefit should be established before the label and the costs are imposed" (Donovan & Cross, 2002, p. 2). Some students, like Dwayne, have remained in the same reading intervention programs for 2 or 3 years, never really catching up, because the true underlying issue wasn't addressed. "Without very good diagnostic information and/or flexible formative assessment system, our instructional program and student performance will not improve, and RTI will simply be an alternate route to special education placement or to permanent membership in Title I classrooms" (Lipson, Chomskey-Higgins, & Kanfer, 2011, p. 205).

CHANGING THE TRAJECTORY FOR *ALL* READERS

Wesley, Sam, Dwayne, and Lamar were all found to be well below grade level in reading and seemed apathetic toward the world of books and learning. They were already, or were in danger of being, segregated in special education or other intervention programs. However, when Wesley and Sam found a book that was of high interest to them, even though it angered them at times, they became motivated and capable learners. They were delighted to find a departure from worksheets with bland passages, phonics exercises, and multiple-choice comprehension questions. They were fully engaged and in an emotionally safe environment where they could discuss a book from their viewpoint of being Black boys. They were able to assert their linguistic and cultural identity during their comprehension conversation with their teacher, often standing up, pacing back and forth, and passionately vocalizing about the injustices of their past and their promises and hopes for their future. As a result, they were quickly learning to read in a proficient and fluent manner. Best of all, they wanted to read more books like *The Whipping Boy.*

Because Dwayne was not making progress in his Title I classroom for reading, a reading specialist agreed to work with him for a few weeks during his referral and evaluation process. It was found that when he got stuck on words he didn't know, he didn't use any metacognitive strategies, made no appeals for help, and made word substitutions that were visually similar but semantically and structurally incorrect, such as *spared* for *spread*, *published* for *polished*, and *trouble* for *terrible*. In comprehension conversations, he often shrugged his shoulders, explained the gist of a text, and generally showed apathy toward reading. Despite these issues, the reading specialist started Dwayne right off on 5th-grade books, instead of his current level of 3rd-grade books, and on material that would be of high interest to older boys. Whenever Dwayne got stuck on unknown words, he was shown how to read ahead and go back to the unknown words, to make sure the words made sense, and what to do if he didn't know what a word meant. He was shown how to use visual imagery skills to improve his comprehension, and to increase his enjoyment of books. Dwayne improved significantly to the point where he was reading close to targeted level and reading more for pleasure, both at school and at home. Because the intervention met his individual needs, used authentic and interesting material, and aided his significant growth, Dwayne was no longer seen as potentially eligible for special education.

It is not enough to simply expect high standards in a classroom. All students need to be respected as *students* and seen as *learners*. Unfortunately, for some students, particularly Black boys like Wesley and Sam, the primary focus is to maintain discipline and order as opposed to seeing and teaching them as fully capable literacy learners. However, culturally responsive teachers see all students as being truly deserving of an *education*—learning to read and write—and believe all students are expanding on their own linguistic, cultural, and even academic backgrounds. Therefore, in culturally responsive classrooms, every effort is made to minimize overt and covert exclusionary tactics for disciplinary and/or academic reasons. The following list offers thought-provoking questions that can serve as an impetus to support teachers in exploring issues of race.

Listening to the Voices of Race

> *What does your inner voice about race say? Listen to it carefully.*
> *How can you embrace difference in a proactive and positive*
> *manner, replacing any denial, resistance, defensiveness, or fear?*

Teachers who listen to their inner voices about race become culturally responsive teachers. They are able to move outside their comfort zones and away from an environment rooted in the illusion of cultural neutrality and homogeneity. They make deliberate efforts to embrace cultural pluralism and recognize the strengths and rich diversity among their students. They are in a better position to design inclusive classrooms as well as foster collaboration, exploration, expansion, and guidance for all, including students like Wesley, Sam, Dwayne, and Lamar. They are able to make learning relevant to and effective for all students, and in turn, they give students meaningful opportunities to learn that transcend into achievement.

Stepping out of Comfort Zones

Do you carry on courageous conversations in your attempt to explore issues of race in a safe manner with your colleagues?

Intentionally and thoughtfully exploring issues of race is a frightening prospect for many teachers. Conversations that do occur among educators often minimize the role of race in determining equity in our schools and focus instead on issues of poverty, language, family values, or even disabilities without recognizing the role that race plays in these issues. "Even more interesting is how much more important race becomes when boundless energy and effort are placed on suppressing it as a topic of conversation or aspect for analysis" (Singleton, 2013, p. 39). Team members carrying on courageous conversations about race in data analyses may experience a heightened racial consciousness. However, as mutual and collaborative professionals, they should avoid bringing an expectation that colleagues of color should explain, represent, or speak for their population. Instead, all educators should look at systemic structures that perpetuate issues of race—and educators who are part of the dominant White culture should explain these for themselves as well. A strong education team works toward teaching competency in offering linguistically and culturally responsive curriculum and instruction as opposed to taking a view that a certain population needs special help in some sort of special program.

Balancing Race and Colorblindness

There is a fine line between treating students justly, but at the same time, acknowledging issues of racial disparities in schools and the larger society. How can you maintain this balance in your classroom?

In light of the fact that our schools are becoming increasingly diverse, policymakers and educators are at the crucial point of having to accept and even embrace the existence of the cultural pluralism by necessity. Yet, the purpose of schooling is to teach the skills that are necessary for further educational and economic opportunities. Teachers can recognize, respect, and value students as individuals as well as within each cultural group. They can develop culturally responsive classrooms so that multiple literacies can be bridged in a meaningful and purposeful manner so that students can become competent in a variety of situations.

Being Mindful of Generations of Impact

How might your students have been impacted by a persistent lack of educational opportunity? In what ways can you reverse this trend by identifying and building on your students' unique literacy knowledge?

Culturally responsive teachers see that all families care about their children's education. All families have strengths, and even those who may consider themselves "illiterate" have something to contribute to the literacy development of their children. Language and literacy practices occur naturally in every family nationwide. Examples of culturally situated patterns of using print have been well established in ethnographic studies (Heath, 1983; Taylor & Dorsey-Gaines, 1988). Unfortunately, success in school is largely determined by how well the practices at home and in the community match the language and literacy occurring at school. When teachers practice strong listening skills, instead of telling parents what they should or should not do, they can take on an empathetic and supportive role in developing cultural responsive literacy all around.

A Culturally and Linguistically Safe Environment

Beyond making a few multicultural books available in classroom libraries and observing Black History or Hispanic Heritage months, how can your classroom materials, environment, and discussions be made emotionally safe, meaningful, and culturally and linguistically relevant so that all students are included and engaged in literacy activities?

Although *The Whipping Boy* is not what most would consider a "multicultural" text, the discussion among Wesley, Sam, and their teacher about race in response to the book is an example of culturally responsive teaching. But it is only a starting point. Discussions do not by any means—and should not—always have to surround historical injustices, but they should be grounded in positive discourse that validates and affirms cultural heritage and identity. In this country, where racism is still one of the major unresolved social problems, "books may be one of the few places where children who are socially isolated and insulated from the larger world may meet people unlike themselves. If they see only reflections of themselves, they will grow up with an exaggerated sense of their own importance and value in the world—a dangerous ethnocentrism" (Bishop, 1990, p. ix). Much effort is needed to have children's books, classroom materials, and especially discussions become more representative of the diversity in our schools.

Handling Public Judgment and Admonishments

How are you handling public judgment, admonishments, and one-sided opinions about achievement gaps that come your way? How can you advocate for everyone to accept, and even cherish, the diversity in our schools?

Although it is appropriate and necessary to have an open dialogue surrounding the issues of achievement gaps, community members, parent volunteers, politicians, and even teachers are often too quick to judge and offer one-sided opinions, quick-fixes, and even admonishments. It may not be an easy feat, but general education teachers are wise to keep this behavior in check, especially for individual students like Wesley, Sam, Dwayne, and Lamar. Teachers should remind others that there are no easy answers for addressing the achievement gap, disproportionality, or the discipline gap. This is as a gentle way to advocate for everyone in our increasingly diverse society. Because there have been all kinds of "reforms" and initiatives since the early days of desegregation, the real answer may be as unique as individuals themselves. Not only that, but the real answer may lie within the 12 years of close relationships between educators and the students during the school years. Twelve (or 13, if a student attended kindergarten) years of elementary and secondary school with a dozen or so teachers and administrators who have a local and direct impact on the education of a student can make or break that student's opportunity to learn to read and write fluently, which then leads to high academic achievement. When teachers continually guide community members, parent volunteers, and policymakers toward developing positive viewpoints about diversity in their classrooms, they build a trusting environment and are able to reach out to all. Then—and only then—can the local community be assured that there will be a graduating class of fluent readers and effective writers who are ready for their future college and career endeavors.

TAKING OWNERSHIP FOR ALL STUDENTS

Taking ownership for teaching *all* students can be done by changing from an achievement viewpoint to a viewpoint of ensuring appropriate and individualized *opportunities* to learn to read. The "role of special education should be to minimize the impact of a disability and maximize the opportunities for children with disabilities to participate in general education in their natural community" (Hehir, 2005, p. 49). Because of the blurred lines between ableism and racism, I suggest that it would be more helpful to say: The role of an *education team* should be to minimize the impact of (insert your label here, such as *impoverished*, *hyperactive*, *academically low-achieving*, or whatnot) and to maximize the opportunities for students to participate in general education in the natural community. Now is a crucial time to address pervasive ableist and underlying racist beliefs within our school systems, teachers, parents, and community so that we can adhere to the good intentions of the reauthorized Individuals with Disabilities Act.

CHAPTER 6

Reading as an Escape?

THE GAP:
SEEING STUDENTS AS "RELUCTANT" OR
OTHERWISE "USING ESCAPE TACTICS"

Regina, a biracial 4th-grader who spoke African American English as her primary language, was a likable, personable, tomboyish girl. Because of low achievement, she ended up in special education, categorized as a student with an emotional disturbance. When necessary, Regina showed a very strong sense of street smarts and told her teacher that she could fight like a boy for what she thinks is right. However, she was out of school often because of the poverty and alcoholism in her home environment or because she overslept and missed the bus. Even when her attendance improved, Regina was frequently removed from the classroom or suspended from school for being unable to manage her anger. Because Regina couldn't keep pace with the instruction in her class and missed a lot of sessions with her reading intervention teacher, her problems escalated even further. It got to the point where she shared that it was easier to just read and write text messages on her cellphone. For example, in writing *LOL*, she didn't have to worry about reading or spelling *laughing out loud*. To her, there was no point in learning to read and write for school; she was hardly there, never knew what was going on, and couldn't keep up anyway.

THE VIEW OF STUDENTS AS "RELUCTANT"
OR OTHERWISE "USING ESCAPE TACTICS"

Many students, like Regina, come to school with mental, emotional, and/or behavioral difficulties that appear to be barriers to learning to read and write. Many teachers have had students like Regina who appear unable to focus or seem anxious, unmotivated, impulsive, disengaged, reluctant, angry, hard to reach, or misbehaved, or use other escape tactics. Educators face frustrating and difficult situations with these students when they lack the training, support, and understanding of the disciplinary alternatives that they and the students need (Losen & Martinez, 2013). Although 6% of students with disabilities are identified as having an emotional disturbance under the Individuals with Disabilities Act (IDEA) (National Center for Education Statistics, 2014a), between 14% and 20% of young people experience a mental, emotional, and behavioral disorder at a given point in time (O'Connell, Boat, & Warner, 2009). This discrepancy indicates that many students with mental, emotional, or behavioral distress may be unsupported in an academic setting. Although the suspected underidentification of students with emotional disturbances is troubling, the demographic makeup of the students who have been found eligible for special education is equally concerning (Hanchon & Allen, 2013) in that males, students with Black or Brown skin, and those from lower-economic and single-parent homes are more likely to be identified as having an emotional disturbance than their counterparts. No matter what the mental, emotional or behavioral difficulties might be, a common deficit view is taken by educators that students like Regina are disaffected from literacy development because of their personal condition.

As anyone surrounded by an army of young children knows, schools can be a wild world of tantrums, outbursts, and meltdowns. After all, most of us can identify with Max in Sendak's book, *Where the Wild Things Are* (Sendak, 1963), or sympathize with Alexander in Viorst's book, *Alexander and the Terrible, Horrible, No Good, Very Bad Day* (Viorst, 1972). Yet, we know that schools, particularly elementary schools, are places of discipline and quiet study only in a perfect world. How to reach and teach Regina and other students who have adverse childhood experiences or are otherwise in distress is often a bewildering and puzzling process for teachers and administrators.

DEFINING AND ADDRESSING EMOTIONAL DISTURBANCES AND THEIR RELATIONSHIP TO LANGUAGE DISORDERS

Identifying students as emotionally disturbed is a thorny process for psychologists and their special education teams. According to the IDEA, emotional disturbance means a condition in which one or more of the following characteristics is exhibited over a long period of time and to a marked degree that adversely affects a student's educational performance: (1) an inability to learn that cannot be explained by intellectual, sensory, or health factors; (2) an inability to build or maintain satisfactory interpersonal relationships with peers and teachers; (3) inappropriate types of behavior or feelings under normal circumstances; (4) a general pervasive mood of unhappiness or depression; and (5) a tendency to develop physical symptoms or fears associated with personal or school problems. Unfortunately, the task of determining eligibility is complicated for psychologists and special education teams to discern a level of severity that sufficiently constitutes a "marked degree," symptom persistence suggesting an "extended" period of time, and educational impact that qualifies as "adverse." In many instances, the answers to these questions are equivocal and entail subjective decisionmaking on the part of the referral team, particularly the school psychologist (Hanchon & Allen, 2013). Despite much research and many advances in childhood mental and emotional health, the definition of emotional impairment used within federal law hasn't changed in more than 50 years. Therefore, there is risk of over- and underidentification among students who are in mental, emotional, or behavioral distress. This, in turn, has the potential to lead to achievement gaps for such students.

Language development is a key foundation for academic, economic, and social performance. Some students who are believed to have mental, emotional, or behavioral distress may also turn out to have underlying language disorders. Studies have demonstrated high levels of comorbidity among language, literacy, and behavior in clinical populations (Law, Tomblin, & Zhang, 2008). Anxiety, depression, social isolation, and aggressive and rule-breaking behavior can obscure the identification of language impairments (Maggio, Granana, Richaudeau, Torres, Giannotti, & Suburo, 2014). It is likely that four out of five children with emotional or behavior disorders had at least a mild language impairment that escaped the attention of relevant adults (Hollo, Wehby, & Oliver, 2014). Unfortunately, teachers sometimes avoid interacting with students, like Regina, who exhibit the most problematic behavior and instead choose to engage in more instructional interactions with students who exhibit more appropriate behavior (Sutherland & Morgan, 2003). Decreased instruction and scaffolding as a reaction to the circumstances at hand, whether for mental, emotional, or behavior distress, language disorders or any other reason, is a precursor to the achievement gap for these students.

The impact of poverty, stress, and trauma on educational achievement in reading is well documented in both scholarly circles and media outlets. Nationally, between 2000 and 2012, the percentage of people in poverty increased from 12.2% to 15.9% (Bishaw, 2013). More than one in four American working families now earn wages so low that they have difficulty surviving financially (Waldron, 2004). With poverty, there is a heightened risk of childhood behavioral disorders, learning difficulties, and learning disorders, which together have an additive effect on educational outcomes (Howe & Covell, 2013). Schools often use deficit ideology to justify existing conditions, such as the socioeconomic achievement gap, by identifying the problem of inequality as located within, rather than as pressing upon, people who are poor (Gorski, 2012). For example, misperceptions and stereotypes that characterize parents who live in poverty as people who do not value education, as lazy, as substance abusers, or as people whose children are linguistically deprived in turn leads to programs or policies that attempt to "fix" their parenting when they may in fact be caring and attentive parents. Like many parents and caregivers, Regina's mother and grandmother cared deeply about Regina's literacy development and education and demonstrated a strong work ethic despite the poverty, stress, and trauma in their lives. Rather than countering risk factors, schools actually amplify them through the punitive practices of grade retention, corporal punishment, exclusion, and teachers' differential expectations for and behaviors toward students from families with low income (Howe & Covell, 2013). When schools do not promote a consistent, safe, and restorative learning environment for distressed students, students like Regina are more prone to feel reluctant or use escape tactics.

An extensive body of literature has described interrelations and associations among language, literacy, learning, and behavioral problems in school-age children, but causal or directional mechanisms of these relations have yet to be established (Hollo, Wehby, & Oliver, 2014; Law, Tomblin, & Zhang, 2008; Stipek, Newton, & Chudgar, 2010). Labels or broad descriptions that have been attached to students, such as their unreadiness, struggles, special needs, and language differences, can manifest as mental, emotional, or behavioral issues as well. For example, students who are unsupported in their readiness for school or who struggle with reading are more likely to exhibit symptoms of distress because of their unreadiness or struggles in reading. When students are deemed academically unready, struggling, or special needs and are viewed from a deficit viewpoint in the first place, their mental, emotional, and behavioral issues may also go unaddressed, exacerbating the original deficit viewpoint. For Regina, it was the vicious downward cycle of multiple deficit viewpoints and inflexibility throughout her educational career that unwittingly *created* her achievement gaps, which made the gap very difficult her to climb out of.

The chicken–egg conundrum—the circular question of which came first, the behavior or the access to learning—is particularly glaring when schools impose zero-tolerance or other harsh disciplinary policies on students who are in distress. Not only are students suspended from school, but they may also be subjected to in-house suspension or removal from the classroom to take teacher-directed timeouts in hallways for violating school-defined codes. As with Regina, a vast majority of suspensions are for minor infractions of school rules, such as disrupting class, tardiness, and dress-code violations, rather than for serious violent or criminal behavior (Losen & Martinez, 2013). The effectiveness of automatic and exclusionary discipline policies is increasingly questionable (Council on School Health, 2013). The inflexible response to misbehavior practiced in zero-tolerance or "tough-love" environments is actually likely to harm students' futures, undermine teacher–student and teacher–parent relationships, seriously reduce instruction time, and lower overall school performance (Losen & Martinez, 2013). Out-of-school suspension and expulsion can also contribute to the risk of a student dropping out of high school. The costs when a person fails to complete secondary education are significant and are borne by society as a whole (Council on School Health, 2013).

DISTINGUISHING ACHIEVEMENT GAPS VERSUS OPPORTUNITY GAPS

Regina came to school with the odds—poverty, chronic stress, and trauma in her home and community—stacked against her. Educators took a deficit viewpoint, believing that her motivation, engagement, and even behavior were barriers to her learning to read proficiently and write effectively. At the same time, through no fault of her own, Regina had academic risk factors that exacerbated the emotional stress inadvertently created by her school. She was biracial, spoke African American English, was placed in special education, and was frequently removed from her classroom. Despite her street-tough appearance, Regina was lost and underachieving. And she was indeed angry. She wanted her rights—a right to belong, a right to learn.

The Achievement Gap	The Opportunity Gap
Achievement gaps occur when mental, emotional, or behavioral difficulties are seen as barriers to literacy development. This gap is a result of a viewpoint that students in distress, like Regina, must be "cured" or better behaved *before* they can access literacy instruction.	Policymakers and educators attempt to create "safe" schools as an opportunity for all students to learn through the use of zero-tolerance or other discretionary disciplinary policies. However, "opportunities" for individual students in distress take the form of "tough-love" disciplinary approaches or special education placement. This brings further marginalization and a vicious cycle of academic underachievement.

Regina was given frequent "opportunities" to repair her behavior. She was removed from her classroom numerous times through out-of-school suspension, in-house suspension, and even teacher requests to take timeouts in various offices and hallways. She was pulled out for intervention services and even sessions with the school social worker or psychologist. She had more than enough reprimands and lectures, punctuated with threats that if she didn't improve her behavior or attendance, she would fall further behind. Finally, Regina was referred for special education services and placed in a resource room. Unfortunately, this resource room offered "life skills," such as self-care, cooking, and arts and crafts as opposed to literacy and academic instruction. And once she was identified as a student with special needs, Regina found herself facing patronizing treatment and pity. Because the focus was solely on Regina's anger and poor behavior, she had very few opportunities for a safe and restorative environment in which she could learn to read and write and strengthen her literacies. Regina's achievement gap occurred, not because of *her* status as a "troubled" student, but because of ineffective school policies that did not respond to her strong needs for trust, structure, consistency, and emotional safety at school.

The power of teacher language is paramount to creating safe and restorative classroom environment. It doesn't take long for students, particularly those already in mental, emotional, or behavioral distress, to translate frequent removals from the classroom for so-called timeouts into the belief that they are unable to learn to read and write and take part in their educational communities. Language molds our sense of who we are; it helps us understand how we think, work, and play, and it influences the nature of our relationships (Denton, 2007). Students who doubt their competence set low goals, choose easy tasks, and plan poorly when they attempt to complete assignments. When they face difficulties, they become confused, lose concentration, and start telling themselves stories about their own incompetence (Johnston, 2004). Language is a tool that helps teachers articulate a vision, convey their faith that students can attain it, give feedback that names students' strengths, and offer guidance that extends students' skills (Denton, 2007). Lost opportunities become a precursor to the achievement gap when teachers focus on students' poor behavior rather than their abilities, causing students to view themselves based on unsuccessful experiences in literacy development and their education as a whole.

The primary purpose of school is to foster literacy development and provide an education, but school is a setting in which the social-emotional and academic domains are reciprocal and inextricably connected. Children's social behavior can promote or undermine their learning, and their academic performance may have implications for their behavior as well (Miles

& Stipek, 2006). General education teachers have a set of basic behaviors that they deem important for students to learn, such as sitting still, working independently, cooperating with their peers, and listening to the teacher. Too often, when such behaviors are difficult for certain students to manage, this is interpreted immediately as intentional noncompliance or oppositional behavior on the part of the student, instead of a response to linguistic and cultural differences, misunderstanding, sensory overload, or frustration. Although the evidence clearly and consistently supports the view that positive learning-related behavior promotes literacy achievement, there is also some support for the inverse hypothesis—namely, that high achievement leads to an increase in positive learning behavior in the later grades in elementary school (Stipek, Newton, & Chudgar, 2010). Fostering resiliency for all students and teaching them to read proficiently and write effectively within the walls of the schools is something over which educators have control. Unfortunately, although many of Regina's waking hours were spent at school, the inordinate amount of teacher focus on her behavior became an additional source of stress on her life. Whereas blame for her achievement gap was attributed by her teachers to her home and community life, in reality her achievement gap also stemmed from her difficult days at school.

Though schools can indeed be stressful environments for some students, traditional ways of structuring small-group instruction meant to help students like Regina may actually be counterproductive for students in distress. Within each classroom, there has been a large shift in schools to include guided reading groups as an essential element of high-quality literacy education (Fountas & Pinnell, 2012) in an attempt to provide differentiated reading instruction. However, without conscious thought about students' literacy background, instructional needs, and circumstances, guided reading groups can turn out to be just another form of insidious segregation. Regina was placed into a low-level guided reading group that also included another member who was in severe emotional and behavioral distress. Regina's entire group was the most difficult one for their teacher to manage. Her teacher admitted that this group was her least favorite group and that she met with them only once or twice a week because she felt ineffective in reaching out to them.

According to a survey about guided reading practices, teachers predominantly used homogeneous grouping, averaging six students based on developmental levels, when they formed guided reading groups (Ford & Opitz, 2008). When students are divided into reading groups solely based on reading benchmark levels, or even scheduling logistics, some students, like Regina, are at risk of being placed in low-level groups. Furthermore, reading groups tended to remain fairly static (Ford & Opitz, 2008), indicating that educators do not practice dynamic grouping arrangements according to individual need, interest, and growth over time. Guided reading groups, either within or outside of general education, may seem to offer more opportunity for struggling students, but for some students, guided reading groups can be just as fragmented and disconnected as remedial reading programs, leading to the loss of students' opportunities to become proficient and fluent readers.

CHANGING THE TRAJECTORY OF "RELUCTANT" READERS

Regina's early years were stressful for her. Not only did she live in an environment where she experienced poverty and parental substance abuse, but she was also disciplined frequently at school for her inability to manage her anger. Regina eventually became eligible for special education services, classified as a student with an emotional disturbance. However, by 4th grade, it seemed she was finding herself sent to the school office for disciplinary reasons for every minor infraction—many of which were a result of cultural and linguistic misunderstanding on the part of her teacher—as well as for standing up for what she thought was right. Her world spun out of control both at home and at school, and it was not long before she found herself labeled an underachiever in reading and writing.

To change Regina's trajectory, we would need to begin by acknowledging her distress and also embracing her as a student with a strong need for acceptance, structure, consistency, and patience. We would view her as a student fully capable of learning to read and write and becoming a part of her educational community despite her distress. After all, Regina was a bright, talented, and motivated student with quite a wry sense of humor. It was not helpful to Regina for educators to identify her home and community environment as the sole reasons for her emotional disturbance and educational underachievement and then leave it at that. As her social worker pointed out, school can be made a place of emotional safety, one over which educators *do* have control. Teachers may ask themselves the following questions as they move toward eliminating gaps in educational opportunity for students who deal with poverty, stress, and trauma and have a tendency to show reluctance or use escape tactics during literacy instruction.

Taming the Wild World of Emotion and Behavior

What does your inner voice about say about students who are reluctant to engage in the classroom or who misbehave? Listen to it carefully. How can that voice be changed from a tone of negativity about the student to thinking about the kinds of safe and restorative environment you can provide?

Although a basic set of behavioral expectations is necessary to create an environment conducive to learning, teachers need to examine classroom rules and their requests about specific behaviors or language to determine whether such rules are necessary for maintaining the learning atmosphere or if they have more to do with power and control over individual students. Townsend (2000) remarked on the spiraling effect that occurs when teachers expect students to engage in behaviors that the students perceive as meaningless and controlling. The students become oppositional or argumentative, and then the teacher feels justified in resorting to discipline methods that may exclude them from the classroom setting. Regina, while participating in a debate about a text, was indeed standing up, pacing, gesturing, and even speaking in a manner that may have appeared antagonistic or aggressive to her teachers. I would encourage teachers to apply Brenda L. Townsend's (2000) "so-what" test in their attempts to avoid potential biases and inequities while disciplining students (p. 285). So what if a student gets up on his knees and haunches over, or even sprawls on the floor, while reading? So what if a small group of students works cooperatively on an assignment? So what if a student sidles up to join a discussion in a guided reading group? So what if a student wants to read a book at a text level higher or lower than her current reading level? So what if a student asks another for the spelling of a word? So what if a student doodles for a bit while thinking about what to write in a reader's response journal? By practicing the "so-what" test, teachers make clear to all that the growth of students' language and literacies is more important than their behavior.

Managing Our Own Hot Buttons

Are you aware of your own hot buttons when working with students who have strong personalities or are in distress? In what ways can you separate and manage your own feelings and responses from the students'?

Just as there is a wide range of children's mental, emotional, or behavioral difficulties, educators come complete with their own personal hot buttons and emotional baggage and have a range of tolerance for difficulties. When Regina moved to 5th grade, with a new teacher and a fresh start, the stress of school began to decreased for her. Once Regina was placed in a warm, accepting, structured, and consistent classroom environment, her new education team worked closely with her on developing appropriate social behaviors and staying out of trouble. At the same time, they disregarded minor behaviors that had no bearing on her learning or her classroom. In fact, most of Regina's previous disciplinary actions, caused by linguistic and cultural differences between her and her former teacher, were wrongfully magnified by her emotional outbursts. Teachers who are conscious of linguistic and cultural differences between themselves and their students, like Regina's 5th-grade teacher, are able to brush off behaviors that are the norm in another culture, even if those behaviors are seen as unacceptable in their own. As a result, Regina's absences—and her removal and suspension rates—decreased significantly. Although Regina was still reluctant to write, she quickly increased her reading proficiency to the point where she could read text in social studies, science, and math at school as well. She even began to think of science as fun and loved making lab observations using diagrams and tables. She began to escape into the world of books each evening while waiting for her mother and grandmother to return home from work. And because Regina was involved and enjoying school, she also made sure she got to school on time on her own.

Advocating for Students in Distress

Are you taking ownership—and leadership—in advocating for students who are prone to emotional distress so they can be treated in a positive, safe, and restorative manner?

When schools have already given students a deep-seated narrative of poor behavior and underachievement, it does not take much for them to lose hope in their ability to read and learn. Students need to develop a strong sense of trust in their general education teachers without their "problems" simply being passed on to someone else, such as a special educator, counselor, or principal. Most important, they need their teachers' advocacy throughout their entire school day. Regina's 5th-grade teacher forged a consistent and trusting relationship, which increased Regina's participation in school, was crucial to increasing her confidence, and strengthened her literacy. Fifth grade is also when students at Regina's school begin to learn to play a musical instrument. Regina found herself becoming a talented violin player with a distinctive urban beat. She shared that reading music seemed a lot more straightforward than reading books and that she loved practicing violin at home. Music is a viable type of literacy (Hansen, Bernstorf, & Stuber, 2004). Unfortunately, an incident occurred that enraged Regina to the point of throwing her violin, stomping out of the music room, and ultimately on the way to another suspension. Her music teacher disciplined her for forgetting her music book despite her chaotic home environment. Regina couldn't understand why she couldn't just borrow another book for that day because hers was simply at home, not lost forever. In this case, Regina needed her general education teacher to advocate for her success in music as well. A more forgiving approach than one her music teacher took might have had a more positive outcome for both the music teacher and for Regina, as well as for other students in distress. The importance of positive, safe, and restorative environments in *all* areas of language and literacies is paramount for students who come to school with adverse childhood experiences. Regina's strong personality and wit could be quite a source of irritation for a teacher, but on the flip side, could be a positive source of respect for her as a person and as a student.

Fostering Exploration, Collaboration, Expansion, and Guidance

Have you taken the time on a regular basis to step back, with a notepad in hand, and objectively observe your own classroom? Do all students appear to be emotionally safe and fully engaged in literacy activities? If not, how can you create a more flexible classroom environment that meets the needs of all your students?

A subtle form of segregation occurs when teachers maintain a dry climate of direct instruction, including lecturing, providing information, asking questions, checking for correct answers, making assignments, and monitoring for completion. In some cases, this kind of pedagogy is reserved only for certain groups of students within a class because they are not able read or write as efficiently as their peers. However, this kind of teaching reduces expectations and promotes an atmosphere characterized by compliance and resistance, rather than one of exploration, collaboration, expansion, and guidance for all. Ultimately, teachers and resistant students may develop an unstated deal in which the students won't disrupt the class in exchange for not being asked to participate in certain activities. These are the students (like Regina) who remove themselves to the back row, pull hoodies over their heads, or otherwise quietly hang about in the margins of the classroom. Haberman (1991) noted that discipline and control are primarily a *consequence* of teaching and not a *prerequisite* condition of learning. Therefore, when inclusive teachers ensure a high level of exploration, collaboration, expansion, and guidance during language and literacy instruction, emotional and behavioral problems are likely to decline or even disappear altogether.

READING AS AN ESCAPE

Adverse childhood experiences, poverty, behavior, and language and literacy are inextricably connected and complex. Schools actually create additional stresses when they view students in distress through deficit viewpoints. Special education referrals or strict disciplinary policies might seem to provide educators with opportunities to respond to unacceptable behaviors. However, these measures can also set the stage for an achievement gap. By creating a warm, accepting, and structured climate of inclusion for all, a general education teacher is in the best position to support students in their exploration of language and literacies, no matter where they are or what they bring to school. After all, reading should be a source of pleasurable escape from chronic or acute stress.

CHAPTER 7

Reading the Fine Print of Tests

THE GAP:
STUDENTS WHO "FAIL" TO MAKE THE GRADE

Carter, a 4th-grader from a homeless family, didn't pass the state test with proficiency, was a year behind grade level on a benchmark assessment, and scored low on a computerized reading test. Carter couldn't grasp some of the passages on these tests. One test item happened to be about clamming along the seashore. Being from among the corn in the Midwest, Carter had absolutely no background knowledge on clamming or seashores. He didn't even know that clams could be eaten as food. It was all very confusing to him. Even so, Carter was a happy student. He never complained about school, was always cooperative and willing to do his assignments, and even enjoyed reading. His teacher observed that he had appropriate cueing strategies for decoding unknown words and adequate fluency, even on texts considered to be at his grade level. Carter showed interest in everything his teacher provided for him to read and confronted only a few new vocabulary words here and there. There was a significant difference between Carter's relative success in the classroom and his test scores. Yet, he was brought to a special education referral team because of underachievement on his assessment scores.

Like Carter, in the same grade, Ramie had low reading scores that concerned her teachers and they suggested that she might need special education. Unlike Carter, she was from an affluent family and was surrounded by books, journals, and newspapers. It was thought that she might have dyslexia because she kept reversing letters and whole words, such as *for* versus *from* and *was* versus *saw*. She also made reading miscues that didn't make sense in context, such as *covered* versus *carved*. She tried to sound out every letter and every word regardless of whether the words made sense to her. Phonics was her weakest link but the very link that she worked the hardest at. After several weeks of reading intervention, Ramie began to use structural and semantic cues to support her decoding and comprehension.

The intervention that Ramie received helped her because it focused on her strengths, rather than on phonics. Assignments and tests with decontextualized words were so challenging and didn't allow her to display the reading progress that she had made. On a district-assigned computerized test, she read a passage about the tools one needed for a project, such as a rake, shovel, hoe, and some seeds. The question after this particular passage required students to determine which word defined the project and offered four multiple-choice items. Ramie ruled out two easily and was left with the words *garage* and *garden*. Because she was weak in phonics and these words were presented in isolation, and because she had no other way of using the cueing strategies she had been taught, Ramie became bewildered. She studied the passage and her two words again. She then turned to her teacher and said, with great clarity, that she knew that the passage was about gardening but she could not choose the correct word. Ramie knew that her progress in reading had improved but was discouraged by her inability to ace this particular test item. Her reading intervention teacher was also dispirited because Ramie had made so much progress but her test results didn't show it.

Even kindergartners are subjected to standardized tests in reading. Logan, duly settled in front of a computer with a pair of headphones on, faced question after question about the alphabet. Finally, he was presented with four multiple-choice pictures: a letter, book, list, and an index card with a recipe written on it. He was asked which picture could be read to help cook food. A teacher happened to observe him thinking aloud through this test item. First, he exclaimed that he and his dad don't cook, but that his grandma does. He pointed to the recipe card and remarked that Grandma has a bunch of those. He went on to say, pointing at the picture of the list, that his dad uses that when they go to the store. He then pointed to the book and said that his grandma sometimes uses that. (After all, cookbooks look like books.) Finally, Logan decided on the letter because his grandma once sent a letter to his dad with directions for cooking things. He remembered the letter with great fondness, because he and his father took the letter to the store and then came home to cook together. A student as young as Logan, who has no concept of the purposes of testing, will answer tests based on their own experiences and current thought processes, not on what they think might be the correct answers that adults expect of them. Moreover, to the teacher who was listening to his reasoning, he came up with "correct" answers; he understood the question and answered it logically within a context that made sense to him. Standardized tests simply do not have the capacity to accurately assess the complexities of students' reasoning on literacy questions like this one.

Carter, Ramie, and Logan, like many students, are given multiple assessments, benchmarks, and tests for many reasons. Some reasons are to hold schools accountable for student achievement and other reasons are to make instructional decisions about individual students. However, by observing individual students taking tests, teachers have a much more nuanced and valuable idea of a particular student's skills and weaknesses. Observation, along with knowing how tests work, is a key to addressing the issue of opportunity gaps for students. Carter, Ramie, and Logan would be at risk for losing valuable instructional time with their general education teachers if their test scores placed them in remedial or intervention services or special education.

STUDENTS WHO ARE SEEN AS "FAILING"

Every time we observe students like Carter, Ramie, and Logan taking tests, we are left with more questions than answers. Are we testing for strategic reading? Or knowledge about clamming at the seashore? Do we mean to test for comprehension? Or decoding skills within the multiple-choice items? Or working memory skills? What about fluency? Furthermore, the consequences of test results for students like Carter, Ramie, and Logan can be significant, and concerning. Carter was indeed reading and reading proficiently, but he didn't always have the background knowledge common among students from families of the mainstream culture that was often necessary to understand test items and answer them correctly. Ramie, after only a few weeks of reading intervention, was rapidly becoming a flexible and fluent reader, and beginning to read for meaning and even pleasure, yet her test scores reflected none of her improvement. Logan, by all means still very young, used sophisticated reasoning to come up with his answer on the test item about cooking from a recipe. Their opportunities for continuing growth in literacy would be at risk if they were referred for a separate reading program or special education based solely on their test scores, and they might begin their educational career with low expectations of their capabilities as a result. Instead, where standardized testing may be mandated, teachers and reading intervention or special education teachers could note the context within the test answers and observe their students' achievement or comprehension where the tests couldn't. This revealing information can be used as guidance toward purposeful literacy instruction.

QUESTIONS ABOUT THE USEFULNESS OF TESTING TO
EVALUATE STUDENT PROGRESS IN LITERACY

Though defining and constructing relationships between standards, assessments, and accountability is complex, just about all students in schools are subjected to testing, especially in reading. Accountability, the process of evaluating school performance on the basis of student performance measures in education, could be addressed in many ways. It is implemented as a political process to ensure democratic accountability, introducing market-based reforms to increase accountability to parents and students, or it is used to increase the professional accountability of teachers (Figlio & Loeb, 2011). Although the purpose for policymakers is to assess, reward, and sanction schools and school districts for the purpose of increasing student achievement, testing inadvertently maintains a deficit model of education, results in overzealous referrals of students for intervention services and special education, and limits opportunities for some students.

In education policy and research, it is common to work with disaggregated achievement data showing patterns, trends, and gaps by specific subgroups of students. Traditionally underperforming groups of students, including students moving in and out of districts as migrants, homeless students, and English language learners, and those with disabilities, are often excluded from accountability because of the unfair challenges teachers and schools face in educating these students. Yet there is trade-off in excluding students on the basis of classification. Exclusion provides schools with less incentive to support these students as well as an incentive to selectively reclassify or move students in order to look better against performance metrics (Figlio & Loeb, 2011). Though it is disheartening when schools maintain a 2-inch binder full of disaggregated data but the local newspaper prints a simple "grade"—a vast oversimplification, awarded to the various schools in a 2-by-4-inch space—it is equally disheartening when persons from underperforming subgroups see their students mentioned in the news media as part of the problem. Furthermore, disaggregating data by population subgroups risks reinforcing to educators and policymakers the notion that certain subgroups have pathological needs, particularly in special education. It risks normalizing the underachievement as something to be expected for individual students simply because they belong to the subgroup under scrutiny.

Assessments are also used to determine if a student is eligible for remedial or intervention services or special education, which in turn, brings another set of challenges and consequences to students. Even though routine IQ testing of students has largely disappeared, sorting and selecting students has continued, and it now relies on achievement tests rather than aptitude tests (Haertel & Herman, 2005). Furthermore, students can be given a quick screening assessment so that data are gathered *before* instruction to determine which students may require further (diagnostic) assessment (Wixson & Valencia, 2011). Screens are generic, quick, and easy to administer to large numbers of students, but they rarely provide enough information to determine the most appropriate intervention or instruction. Unfortunately, based on cut scores from simple screenings, students are typically given an expedient and direct route to reading intervention. Johnson, Jenkins, and Petscher (2010) call into question the use of this direct route approach because their study demonstrated that cut scores based on single measures do not yield the desired accuracy for instructional or intervention decisions. Making decisions solely based on test results, *without* qualitative observations and careful diagnoses of instructional needs, may inadvertently create opportunity gaps for students in reading. This practice sorts students into groups or tiers, each with its own level of curricular expectation, whether the students actually need it or not. It may also place students into reading programs that work on narrow subsets of skills, such as phonics or sight words, which may or may not be necessary or helpful for a particular student. Some students have been retested on the same test over and over again, seemingly with very little progress, and as a result, they remain stuck in specific reading programs that may not serve their best interests.

Supporters of standards, assessment, and accountability argue that these practices create opportunities for students by raising expectations and providing extra instructional support. However, the disconnect between rhetoric and reality is one of the reasons in the 20-year history of standard-based education reforms have failed (Shepard, 2009). Because schools must survive in a climate in which there is an emphasis on test scores and meeting statistical norms, the competitive and conformist nature of schooling may actually exacerbate the original problems for students who are struggling or otherwise in distress (Stoughton, 2006). Furthermore, as the nation and our schools become increasingly culturally and linguistically diverse, not all students will be familiar with the content of some test items. Carter didn't have background about clamming along the seashore, but he knew that he didn't know about those things. Certainly, Carter could learn more about clamming through reading and discussions, but the test was based more on what he happened not to know than on his actual reading skills or his capability to learn. In fact, as a result of the test question, Carter became very interested about the concept that some clams are edible; he asked his teacher where he could find them and whether they would really taste good. Although it is appropriate for our schools to broaden concepts, expand background knowledge, and otherwise enrich the literacy of our students, it is not fair to *test* them without ever giving them the opportunity to become familiar with or learn about concepts that are missing from their background knowledge.

DISTINGUISHING ACHIEVEMENT GAPS VERSUS OPPORTUNITY GAPS

Elected officials, school board members, and the general public, along with parents, teachers, and administrators, have a desire to see students like Carter, Ramie, and Logan achieve well in literacy. Too often, when collecting information about a student, one can easily end up with a repertoire of test scores, but never an adequate picture of that student's reading processes and progress. Accountability as we know it now is not helping our schools because its measures are too narrow and imprecise, and its consequences are too severe (Ravitch, 2011). Too many accountability systems maintain the status quo of sorting students into tiers or tracks, thus maintaining covert and insidious forms of segregation. In contrast, a good assessment system can inform instruction and intervention in an individualized, short-term, and purposeful manner.

The Achievement Gap	The Opportunity Gap
It is often thought that testing actually creates opportunities for schools and students by raising expectations or providing extra instructional support. However, students who *fail* are then considered *unready*, *struggling*, or even *learning disabled*.	When high-stakes decisions are made solely based on test scores, *without* a careful diagnosis of students' instructional needs, it may inadvertently create opportunity gaps for students in reading, in that they are given a direct route to reading intervention or even special education referrals.

Achievement gaps place the burden of passing achievement tests on individual students regardless of where they are in their exploration of literacy. Opportunity gaps are created when teachers and administrators make high-stakes decisions based on imprecise measurement tools and arbitrarily sort students into groups that shape their potential for literacy growth, often negatively.

Opportunity gaps are created for students when the insufficiency of test scores are not recognized. As evidenced by Carter, Ramie, and Logan's experiences, none of these standardized tests is a precise instrument; therefore; these tests can be misleading as a way of diagnosing students' literacy achievement. Teachers will regularly see one student's test scores fall all over the map. Educational psychology is concerned with how students learn and develop in school settings. Attempting to quantify and use mathematical statistics in educational psychology is not an exact science; because it is unethical to manipulate and experiment with students, only causal and correlational relationships between variables can be inferred. Although tests have a range of statistical validity, reliability, bias, scaling, and standard setting, test scores usually do not provide a direct and complete measure of educational achievement (Koretz, 2008). These tests can measure only a subset of the goals of education. Thus, a 3rd-grader who passes a phonics test with ease does not necessarily read fluently at a 3rd-grade level. The test would only be informative and helpful if it tested specifically for the 3rd-grader's knowledge of phonics. Additionally, any kind of scientific test needs to have an accepted number of trials to make sure the result is statistically significant. A test that has only two questions on the alphabet is less predictive of a student's letter knowledge than a test with, say, 50 questions. But realistically, one can only test a young and active kindergartner like Logan for so long in one sitting.

There is also a high rate of random error in educational measurement. Children, being children, get sleepy, hungry, or sick; they shut down emotionally; or they become careless and take guesses. Sometimes there are also external factors, such as noise levels, lighting, or interruptions. One year, during Ramie's state-mandated testing window, the seasonal flu knocked out more than half of the students, many of whom had to face the test while they were still recovering. The next year, Ramie's school fire alarm was accidentally tripped right in the middle of a district test, sending everyone outside, bringing on the fire trucks, and creating quite a bit of excitement.

Because the definition of literacy falls within the realm of politics (Venezky, Wagner, & Cilberti, 1990), some tests, particularly those that determine whether students have learned a specific body of knowledge, are politically motivated. Groups of policymakers and educators decide on standards that reflect their views of what ought to be taught, and either design or purchase tests to ascertain that students have met these outcomes. If there are significant mismatches between the expectations inherent in tests, standards, school curriculum, students' cultural and linguistic environments, and students' reading strengths and weaknesses, then students like Carter, Ramie, and Logan are likely to fail.

CHANGING THE TRAJECTORY OF STUDENTS
WHO "FAIL" STANDARDIZED TESTS

Carter, Ramie, and Logan found themselves placed at desks with sharpened pencils or sitting in front of computers being tested on their reading achievement. All three put effort and thought into the tasks at hand. Carter knew that he was confused about clamming and asked questions to further his background knowledge. Ramie knew that her passage was about gardening. And Logan knew that a letter, book, list, and index card can all be used to help cook food. Yet, all three students were considered "underachieving" or "failing" and were viewed as at-risk for joining a separate remedial reading or special education group. To change the trajectory of their educational careers, teachers should view these students as strengthening their exploration of language and literacies, regardless of what their test scores report. On the one hand, it is necessary to hold educators accountable for providing optimal learning opportunities for their students. On the other hand, our instructional practices need to be tailored to individual students' strengths and weaknesses in a relevant and responsive way in order to address the range of differences that students bring into the classroom (Milner, 2010). Educators and schools should be held accountable for making sure all students learn to read, but testing *alone* will not fairly portray the qualities of a school, a teacher, or patterns of literacy strengths and weaknesses in students. Teachers can be held accountable by their ability to provide authentic and challenging literacy curriculum in which *all* students learn from. Teachers can also be held accountable in their ability to observe, document in running records, and know students as individual language and literacy learners. Following are questions and actions to support educators as they move toward developing professional and objective expertise on issues surrounding assessments and testing materials.

Taking on the View of Growing Students

What does your inner voice say about students who fail to make the grade on standardized tests? Listen to it carefully. How can you avoid thinking of low test scores as evidence of failure or underperformance and ask instead what you can do in a proactive and positive manner to accurately assess students' learning in order to provide context for their test scores?

When teachers refrain from buying into concepts of "underachievement" and "failure" in interpreting standardized test scores, they can view, and help parents, colleagues, and administrators to view, that all students *are* growing as readers and writers. There is a distinction between assessment *of* learning and assessment *for* learning (Stiggins & Chappuis, 2006). An assessment *of* learning is a form of testing or benchmarking, denoting whether a student has achieved or failed to achieve a curricular standard or literacy level. An assessment *for* learning, such as running records or documented observations, is used to inform teachers and students the next steps for instruction. When assessment *for* learning is emphasized, students and their teachers become partners in the classroom assessment process, relying on student-involved assessment, record-keeping, and communication to help students understand what success looks like, see where they are now, and learn to close the gap between the two. Both students and their teachers benefit from having clear purposes and targets when assessing reading and writing development. Once teachers have a clear idea of where all their students are in their individual exploration of literacy, both students and teacher will know how to further improve each student's literacy.

Managing Data

Have you embraced the times by becoming "assessment literate"? Do you have a basic understanding of educational measurement, test design, reliability, validity, and statistics? How are you astute in interpreting results from the various types of assessments and tests to inform your instruction? How do you develop measurable goals for some of your students, with a baseline and target, along with keeping a record of progress?

In developing assessments *for* learning, teachers have a repertoire of personalized assessment tools and they make goals concrete and clear for individual students. The use of tests for reasons other than their intended purpose leads to opportunity gaps. For example, the use of criterion-referenced tests (a test *of* learning), particularly end-of-unit or chapter tests, for the purpose of monitoring progress is inconsistent and does not adequately monitor or ensure growth in literacy. One test might cover words that contain suffixes involving tense and plurals and another might cover understanding of idioms. Both are testing totally different concepts. If a student didn't pass one or the other, he or she might not be monitored in the future for growth and understanding in that specific area. Such one-time tests only serves to denote whether a student passed or failed and does not ensure opportunities for learning. Assessment used for monitoring progress, on the other hand, tests the same concept until the student has achieved it. For example, for students who need to make sure they are making sense of what they are reading by correcting any miscues on their own, taking a running record on a weekly basis can note the number of errors they self-corrected versus the number of errors not self-corrected and show whether the self-correction rate has increased after instruction or intervention.

Another insidious contribution to opportunity gaps is when educators misunderstand or misuse the statistical components of tests. For example, some commercially made progress-monitoring tests in reading not only feature percentile rankings for scores but also include typical rates of improvement over time. Tests having statistics on rates of improvement show that a low score will have a certain, often low, rate of improvement based on their research studies. This information could cause educators to lower their expectations for some students. To illustrate, a kindergartner who ranked in the 10th percentile on a letter identification test would be expected to have a rate of improvement of 0.25 letters per week, which amounts to 1 new letter every 4 weeks. Another kindergartner ranking in the 90th percentile on the same test would be expected to improve by 0.53 letters per week, amounting to 1 new letter in just under 2 weeks. This may be informative but there is no reason to limit kindergartners to learning 1 letter a week or every 4 weeks. They should be given the opportunity to learn about letters in an authentic, holistic, and timely manner, regardless of what percentile rank they happened to fall in.

Developing a Sense of Assessment Literacy

A single test score rarely shows an accurate picture of a student's overall reading ability. Do you know what skill/s each assessment is specifically measuring? Are you aware of any cultural and linguistic biases inherent in the test? What other kinds of assessment or information can you use to inform your instruction?

Although information from carefully chosen test scores can be revealing, classroom teachers also know, through observation and professional judgment, their students' individual strengths and weaknesses in reading. What do students do when they are stuck on an unknown word? How is their fluency? Is it smooth with good inflection or halting, word-by-word reading? Is there depth to your comprehension conversations with them, and are they able to make any personal connections to the text? Are there issues with their attention, stamina, and motivation? Has the students' visual and hearing acuity been checked? What kinds of books do the students like to read? (Lipson, Chomskey-Higgins, & Kanfer, 2011).

Likewise, tests that are not culturally or linguistically sensitive may bring about opportunity gaps for students who may be good readers after all, but may have little or no background knowledge on the topics covered by particular test items. Carter, who was stumped by the concept of clamming at the seashore, was an example of this bias. Indeed, "affluent children are advantaged because their background is similar to that of the test makers, so they are comfortable with the vocabulary and subtle subcultural assumptions of the test" (Loewen, 2007, p. 208). No student should become a victim of opportunity gaps as a direct result of imprecise, biased, or misused testing instruments.

Tailoring Assessments in Relevant and Responsive Ways

How do assessment results impact your instructional or intervention decisions regarding your students? Are your decisions based on multiple sources of information, including observations, running records, and your professional judgment? How can you respond to concerned parents and stakeholders about students' test results?

Opportunity gaps also occur when policymakers and educators use tests that work against the grain of well-rounded reading strategies, as occurred with Ramie's weakness in decoding words in isolation. The multiple-choice test that gave no contextual clues discriminated against Ramie, not to mention it was demoralizing for her. Her parents were disappointed in her and pushed even harder for her to improve her phonetic skills. Her teacher found justification for a special education referral so that Ramie could be diagnosed as having dyslexia and could get extra help in a resource room. In the meantime, everyone lowered their expectations for her, provided her with easier reading material, and placed her in a low-level reading group. When Ramie's parents and teacher were shown qualitative assessments and observations, including running records and miscue analyses over time, they were able to see Ramie in a more positive light as a growing reader. Teachers who closely support their students' growth in literacy also document and share information about that growth with their students, their parents, and stakeholders.

Taking back Ownership and Leadership

Are you taking ownership—and leadership—in interpreting your students' assessment and test results? Are you making collaborative decisions with reading intervention teachers,

*reading coaches, and special education teachers without
simply passing your students who appear to be "failing" on to
someone else?*

Many schools have adopted universal screening programs, such as the use of
1-minute oral reading fluency tests, in which all students are assessed in order to identify students at-risk for further difficulty in literacy development.
Problems with one-time, brief universal screening have been documented
widely across fields of investigation and raise fundamental questions about
whether schools can allocate costly intervention services on the basis of such
screenings (Fuchs & Vaughn, 2012). "Screening measures designed to identify struggling students are usually quite general or sample only a snippet of
skilled reading performance" (Lipson, Chomskey-Higgins, & Kanfer, 2011,
p. 204). Like the quest for the best program to teach reading, "the search for
the one best approach for screening may be unrealistic" (Jenkins, Hudson,
& Johnson, 2007, p. 599). There is serious possibility for error; false nega-
tives or false positives are likely to occur in making instructional decisions
(Valencia, Smith, Reece, Li, Wixson, & Newman, 2010). Furthermore,
when these screenings lead to just one instructional option, are they depriv-
ing poor readers of the individually tailored instruction they are more likely
to receive instead (Fuchs, Mock, Morgan, & Young, 2003)? Despite the use
of screenings, teachers can advocate for keeping students in their general
education classrooms for literacy instruction as much as possible.

Pausing to Take Stock

> *Many tests are given to the entire class at once. Have you,
> with a notepad in hand, objectively observed some of your
> students taking these tests? What kinds of responses are they
> making? Are they taking the test seriously? Do test items with
> multiple-choice answers appear more difficult or easier than
> open-ended questions? Do the test items contain cultural and
> linguistic biases?*

When teachers observe students taking tests, they gain much more information about students' thought processes and literacy knowledge, as was the
case with Carter, Ramie, and Logan. Although it's important to observe students taking tests, a danger is that the lens may become too closely focused
on a particular student; it is important to use observations to focus on the
student's strengths, not just on weaknesses. There is also a danger when assessments—particularly those involving phonics, phonemic awareness, and

oral reading rates, rather than curriculum standards—drive what elementary school literacy programs teach. (Goodman, 2006; Pearson, 2006). Using tests not only as a resource for instruction but to support deficit viewpoints can contribute to opportunity gaps. However, by observing students taking tests, teachers can arrive at a better understanding of how to support their students. Furthermore, by documenting what actually occurs for some students in testing situations, we can determine how well a particular test reflects a student's strengths.

READING THE FINE PRINT

Regardless of which tests are used in schools, most often they create more questions than definitive answers. Because tests do not always reflect school or teacher quality or student ability, and because the sole use of test scores in making high-stakes decisions contributes to opportunity gaps in many ways, educators should develop a strong sense of assessment literacy. Students deserve to be observed so that teachers know how they processed their answers to the test items instead of just what their answers were. Furthermore, just as reading instruction should be individually tailored for different students, assessment data should reflect the instruction and should inform teachers of individual progress.

Reading Right Side Up

Throughout this book, I've shared my experiences with students who were *reading upside down* because of devastating opportunity gaps in their elementary school years. Their opportunity gaps in learning to read proficiently and fluently were a result of subtle political, systemic, and discriminatory barriers, all of which were initially caused by ignorance, attitudes, and judgments. The educational system focused on what was *wrong* with these students, seeing them first and foremost through an ableist lens, identifying them by what they *can't* or *won't* do because of circumstances such as having a medically identified disability, speaking a language other than English, being impoverished or homeless, and so forth. In addition, the students were asked to meet particular expectations regarding the academic level at which they must perform or the way in which the must behave in order to access the education in our schools. If they did not meet those expectations, they were given a range of "opportunities" in the form of special or alternative education such as special education, Title I services, English as Second Language (ESL) classes, reading intervention, and other support programs, often characterized by reduced expectations and a tendency toward instruction in isolated and fragmented skills, which inadvertently creates more roadblocks to proficiency and fluency in reading and writing in many students. If these students had not been given a true opportunity to learn to read proficiently and fluently, they would be at risk for *reading upside down* throughout their school career.

Therefore, this book has consistently stressed the importance of providing opportunities so that *individual* growth in reading and writing is ensured, embraced, and honored in purposeful and positive ways. Furthermore, this book has emphasized the importance of ascertaining whether interventions are meeting the particular instructional needs of each individual student. If they are not, it is crucial to find an intervention tailored specifically to each student's particular level of literacy. Again, all students should learn to read and write *despite* the circumstances they bring to school and should not face limitations *because* of their circumstances.

Because students are taught to read and write by those close to them—their parents, classroom teachers, and perhaps a special education teacher, reading intervention teacher, or mentor—these adults need to take responsibility and accountability for ensuring that students receive a high-quality literacy instruction. Lofty policies, specialized reading programs, and standardized testing have been developed and mandated in response to contentious discussion among educational researchers, educational policymakers, politicians, community members, and the news media about resolving issues of equity, the achievement gap, disproportionality, and the discipline gap in schools for many decades—with little success. Because there is no single answer or single reading instruction method or even single test that reaches all students, teachers and principals need to be given the opportunity to use professional judgment in their own schools. As teachers take back ownership and leadership over their students' progress, they can continue to utilize the support of reading teachers or consultants who have expertise in using a range of instructional and assessment techniques, appropriate resources, and adequate time for collaboration in order to see that all students, albeit in individualized ways, reach a common core of curriculum standards.

Given our increasingly diverse population; the proliferation of information from the Internet that must be read, analyzed, and critiqued; and more demands for a globally competitive and highly skilled workforce, the time is now to ensure that each student becomes a fluent reader and effective writer. Each student *can* become a reader and writer, and even highly literate, despite the following circumstances:

- being unready for kindergarten
- being inadequately taught how to read in 1st through 3rd grade
- having a medically identified disability
- speaking another language instead of or in addition to English
- speaking a variation of English, such as African American English
- having a speech and language disorder
- having Black or Brown skin
- being a reluctant or otherwise misbehaving student
- being impoverished or homeless
- having parents who prefer not to become involved with a formal schooling context or lack academic literacy
- being subjected to standardized tests with dubious results for high-stakes decisionmaking

The unifying theme in each chapter has been the pervasive issue of ableism and continued, but now covert, forms of segregation. The students portrayed in each chapter represent structural and systemic problems that many other students face. Of course, although these issues are far from intentional, they still call for courageous conversations about how we can truly ensure that all of our students are given the opportunity to become literate.

Jenna, the student I mentioned in the Preface, found herself with a huge opportunity gap in learning to read by 4th grade. She had several points against her. She was "unready" for kindergarten, did not have adequate reading instruction between 1st and 3rd grade, was considered to have a medically identified disability (ADD), and had not been given a thorough diagnosis of her reading strengths and weaknesses, all of which contributed to ableism and segregation in her young life. Right from the start, her playing field was not level. It wasn't until I started working with her that she finally started to read *right side up*. Because she had been so focused on letters and words that she lacked reading comprehension, I taught her to use other strategies while reading real books. I showed her how she could read ahead and return to the unknown word, look at the initial sounds or find smaller words within long words, and think about what would make sense. After learning these strategies, Jenna—who was no longer reading on kindergarten level—read aloud to me the following passage from *You Can't Eat Your Chicken Pox, Amber Brown* (Danziger, 1995) on her last day of school before the summer break:

> Third grade.
> Here today.
> Gone tomorrow.
> I can hardly believe it.
> It seems like just yesterday was the first day of school.
> New pens, pencils, erasers, notebooks, clothes, a brain that had a
>   chance to take a break over summer vacation . . . all of the things a
>   kid needs to start a new school year.
> Now it's the last day of school . . . just in time.
> My pens are out of ink. My pencils are stubs. My erasers are all
>   erased. My clothes are getting too small and my brain needs to take
>   a break over summer vacation.
> It's definitely time for school to end. (pp. 1–2)

Jenna read this passage quite proficiently until she got stuck on the word *definitely* in the last line. Using the edge of her bookmark as a guide, she couldn't remember how the syllables were to be divided: *def / in / it / ely*, *de / fin / ite / ly*, or *def / in / i / tel / ly*. She had suddenly regressed to using phonics as her sole means of decoding unknown words, and was again so focused on letters and words that she lost all meaning. I cleared my throat with a little *ahem* as a reminder of what I had taught her. Jenna read ahead, returned to the word, looked at the first three letters, and thought about what would make sense: *It's def . . . def . . . def . . . in . . . definitely time for school to end.* She looked up at me with exasperated laughter and re-marked, "It's *definitely* time for school to end!"

It is also definitely time for gaps in opportunity to end. The following keywords were paramount throughout each chapter in this book bringing a call for change.

Ownership

First off, contrary to what policymakers may assert, it is well recognized that there is no single instructional technique or standardized test that will reach all students. Ownership for closing opportunity gaps belongs on a personal and local level—among the very adults who are immediately sur-rounding the students as they learn to read and write.

Expertise

Teachers must know what proficient and fluent readers look like and make every assurance that struggling readers become good readers in a timely man-ner. They must begin with a good set of diagnostic tools and assessments. They should not rely solely on broad screening and standardized test scores. Using diagnostic information, they must develop an intervention program that meets the individual needs of each student, making appropriate choices from a wide range of techniques. Furthermore, they must ascertain that their intervention is indeed purposeful and effective for their students.

Inclusion

All students belong in classrooms, including those with disabilities and di-verse languages and life experiences. This is not intended to minimize the role of special education, Title I, English as Second Language (ESL), and reading intervention teachers; rather, I simply suggest that support for stu-dents learning to read and write should be thoughtfully connected to what is offered in the general education classroom. The role of these specialized teachers is to provide support to the general education teachers as opposed to providing therapeutic support to individual students and operating in a vacuum. Of course, there are many circumstances where students may need individualized or small-group sessions outside of the classroom, but that the support should be closely tied to the goals of the general education teacher. Most of the time, it is not necessary to replace a well-rounded language and literacy rich curriculum that includes hearing adults read aloud, shared reading among peers, independent reading, and small-group guided reading lessons along with an assortment of the type of word work and writing activities that typify many general education programs.

Universal Design

Inclusion goes hand in hand with universal design. In education, universal design includes multiple ways of presenting information to students, allowing students to demonstrate what they have learned, and engaging their interest and motivation. Universal design does not water down the curriculum standards but instead allows all students to strive for them. Though most students can learn to read and write, not all will learn in the same manner. Some students may need to use large print, and others may need to sit comfortably on a beanbag chair or lie on the floor to read. Some may need more support with decoding and others may need to strengthen their comprehension. Some may need time for independent reading and others may need an adult to read to them. Providing accommodations as an additional component to universal design can allow students to have individualized means toward achieving the standard that is expected for all students. When both inclusion and universal design open up opportunities, achievement goes beyond what most educators and parents would expect. It not only benefits those with disabilities, but also students from diverse cultural and linguistic backgrounds *and* general education students without disabilities.

Authentic and Engaged Reading

When ownership, expertise, inclusion, and universal design are fully in place for all students, opportunities for authentic and engaged reading abound. I know it is possible. I have seen it in many well-organized and quality classrooms throughout my career. However, it did not come easily for the teachers in those classrooms. Teachers need to be given the opportunity to teach with expertise, flexibility, collaboration, and, yes, accountability.

Watching for Ableism

Although many students bring challenging circumstances to the classroom, such as a disability, another language, homelessness, or whatnot, none of these should be the sole reason for their failure to learn to read. There is danger in seeing "special education" students or "struggling" or "at-risk" readers as needing a specialized—and often segregated—program. We are wise to catch inner voices in ourselves that say the words *can't, won't,* or *needs.* Instead, as H. Richard Milner (2011), in the *Harvard Education Letter,* wrote, "Teachers have to ask themselves: *Am I prepared to recognize talent, potential talent, intellect, skill, excellence, and ability when they emerge in an unexpected social context or with an unexpected group of students?*" Changing the focus from what is *wrong* with these students to what they *can* and *will* do in school is one step toward ensuring opportunities for literacy instruction. Of course, we need to acknowledge the circumstances the students bring, but only in objective and supportive ways. Then and only then will schools begin to stop perpetuating the problems of society by unwittingly blurring ableism with issues of race, ethnicity, language, class, gender, and ability within their walls. And then there will be hope that most *all* students can move from *reading upside down* to *reading right side up.*

References

Adams, M. (1998). The three-cueing systems. In J. Osborn & F. Lehr (Eds.), *Literacy for all: Issues in teaching and learning* (pp. 73–99). New York, NY: The Guilford Press.

Allington, R. (2002). What I've learned about effective reading instruction from a decade of studying exemplary elementary classroom teachers. *The Phi Delta Kappan, 83*(10), 740–747.

Allington, R. (2006). Research and the three-tier model. *Reading Today, 23*(5), 20.

Allington, R. (2011). What at-risk readers need. *Educational Leadership, 68*(6), 40–45.

Allington, R. (2013). What really matters when working with struggling readers. *The Reading Teacher, 66*(7), 520–530.

American Association for Applied Linguistics. (2011). *Resolutions*. Available at http://www.aaal.org/content.asp?contentid=137

Aron, L., & Loprest, P. (2012). Disability and the education system. *The Future of Children, 22*(1), 97–122.

Aud, S., Wilkinson-Flicker, S., Kristapovich, P., Rathbun, A., Wang, X., & Zhang, J. (2013). *The condition of education 2013*. Washington, DC: National Center for Education Statistics.

Auerbach, E. (1989). Toward a social-contextual approach to family literacy. *Harvard Educational Review, 59*(2), 165–180.

Barton, P. E., & Coley, R. J. (2009). *Parsing the achievement gap II*. Princeton, NJ: Educational Testing Service.

Barton, P. E., & Coley, R. J. (2010). *The Black-White achievement gap: When progress stopped*. Princeton, NJ: Educational Testing Service.

Bauer, E., & Gort, M. (2012). Reflections and directions for biliteracy research. In E. B. Bauer & M. Gort (Eds.), *Early biliteracy development: Exploring young children's use of their linguistic resources* (pp. 185–191). New York, NY: Routledge.

Berkeley, S., Bender, W. N., Peaster, L. G., & Saunders, L. (2009). Implementation of response to intervention A snapshot of progress. *Journal of Learning Disabilities, 42*(1), 85–95.

Bishaw, A. (2013). *Poverty: 2000–2012*. U.S. Department of Commerce. Washington, DC: U.S. Census Bureau.

Bishop, R. (1990). Mirrors, windows, and sliding glass doors. *Perspectives: Choosing and Using Books for the Classroom, 6*(3).

Blaxland, W. (1996). *Lunch at the zoo*. Sydney, Australia: Scholastic.

Brenner, D., Hiebert, E. H., & Tompkins, R. (2009). How much and what are third graders reading? In E. H. Hiebert (Ed.), *Reading more, reading better: Solving problems in the teaching of literacy* (pp. 188–140). New York, NY: The Guilford Press.

Bridwell, N. (1963). *Clifford the big red dog*. New York, NY: Scholastic.

Brown, A. L., & Donnor, J. K. (2011). Toward a new narrative on black males, education, and public policy. *Race Ethnicity and Education, 14*(1), 17–32.

Buttner, G., & Shamir, A. (2011). Learning disabilities: Causes, consequences, and responses. *International Journal of Disability, Development and Education, 58*(1), 1–4.

Catts, H. W., Fey, M. E., Zhang, X., & Tomblin, J. B. (1999). Language basis of reading and reading disabilities: Evidence from a longitudinal investigation. *Scientific Studies of Reading, 3*(4), 331–361.

Center for Parent Information and Resources. (2012). *Response to intervention*. Available at http://www.parentcenterhub.org/repository/rti/#what

Centers for Disease Control and Prevention. (2014). *Facts about developmental disabilities*. Available at http://www.cdc.gov/ncbddd/developmentaldisabilities/facts.html

Chambers, J. G., Parrish, T. B., & Harr, J. J. (2004). *What are we spending on special education services in the United States, 1999–2000?* Center for Special Education Finance. Washington, DC: American Institutes for Research.

Clay, M. (1979). *Reading begins at home*. Portsmouth, NH: Heinemann.

Clay, M. (1987). *Writing begins at home*. Portsmouth, NH: Heinemann.

Clay, M. (1993a). *An observation survey*. Portsmouth, NH: Heinemann.

Clay, M. (1993b). *Reading recovery: A guidebook for teachers in training*. Portsmouth, NH: Heinemann.

Cochran-Smith, M., & Dudley-Marley, C. (2012). Diversity in teacher education and special education: The issues that divide. *Journal of Teacher Education, 63*(4), 237–244.

Common Core State Standards. (2012). *English language arts standards » Introduction » Key design consideration*. Available at http://www.corestandards.org/ELA- Literacy/introduction/key-design-consideration

Council on School Health. (2013). Policy statement: Out-of-school suspension and expulsion. *Pediatrics, 131*(3), 1000–1007.

Danziger, P. (1995). *You can't eat your chicken pox, Amber Brown*. New York, NY: G. P. Putnam's Sons.

DelliCarpini, M. (2010). Success with ELLs. *English Journal, 99*(6), 93–96.

Denton, P. (2007). *The power of our words*. Turner Falls, MA: Northeast Foundation for Children, Inc.

Donovan, M. S., & Cross, C. T. (2002). *Minority students in special and gifted education*. Washington, DC: National Academies Press.

Dotterer, A. M., Iruka, I. U., & Pungello, E. (2012). Parenting, race, and socioeconomic status: Links to school readiness. *Family Relations, 61*, 657–670.

Elkonin, D. (1963). The psychology of mastering the elements of reading. In B. Simon & J. Simon (Eds.), *Educational psychology in the U.S.S.R.* (pp. 165–179). London, England: Routledge and Kegan Paul Ltd.

Elliott, J. G., & Grigorenko, E. L. (2014). *The dyslexia debate.* New York, NY: Cambridge University Press.

Farran, D. (2011). Rethinking school readiness. *Exceptionality Education International, 21*(2), 5–15.

Fawson, P. C., Ludlow, B. C., Reutzel, D. R., Sudweeks, R., & Smith, J. A. (2006). Examining the reliability of running records: Attaining generalizable results. *The Journal of Educational Research, 100*(2), 113–126.

Ferdman, B. (1990). Literacy and cultural identity. *Harvard Educational Review, 60*(2), 181–204.

Fernald, A., Marchman, V. A., & Weisleder, A. (2013). SES differences in language processing skill and vocabulary are evident at 18 months. *Developmental Science, 16*(2), 234–248.

Ferri, B. A., & Connor, D. J. (2005). Tools of exclusion: Race, disability, and (re) segregated education. *Teachers College Record, 107*(3), 453–474.

Figlio, D., & Loeb, S. (2011). School accountability. In E. A. Hanushek, S. Machin, & L. Woessmann (Eds.), *Handbooks in economics, vol. 3* (pp. 384–417). Amsterdam, The Netherlands: Elsevier B.V.

Finn, C. E., & Petrilli, M. J. (2012). Foreword. In N. Levenson, *Boosting the quality and efficiency of special education.* Washington, DC: The Thomas B. Fordham Institute.

Fisher, D., Frey, N., & Lapp, D. (2012). *Text complexity: Raising rigor in reading.* Newark, DE: International Reading Association.

Fleischman, S. (1986). *The whipping boy.* New York, NY: Greenwillow Books.

Flippo, R. (1999). Redefining the reading wars: The war against reading researchers. *Educational Leadership*, 38–41.

Ford, M., & Opitz, M. F. (2008). A national survey of guided reading practices: What we can learn from primary teachers. *Literacy Research and Instruction, 47*(4), 309–331.

Fountas, I., & Pinnell G. S.(1996). *Guided reading: Good first teaching for all children.* Portsmouth, NH: Heinemann.

Fountas, I., & Pinnell G. S. (2012). Guided reading: The romance and the reality. *The Reading Teacher, 66*(4), 268–284.

Fuchs, D., & Fuchs, L. S. (2009). Responsiveness to intervention: Multilevel assessment and instruction as early intervention and disability identification. *The Reading Teacher, 63*(3), 250–252.

Fuchs, D., Mock, D., Morgan, P. L., & Young, C. L. (2003). Responsiveness-to-intervention: Definitions, evidence, and implications for the learning disabilities construct. *Learning Disabilities Research & Practice, 18*(3), 157–171.

Fuchs, L. S. & Vaughn, S. (2012). Responsiveness-to-intervention: A decade later. *Journal of Learning Disabilities, 45*(3), 195–203.

Gambrell, L. (2011). Seven rules of engagement. *The Reading Teacher, 65*(3), 172–178.

Garcia, O., Kleifgen, J., & Falchi, L. (2008). *From English language learners to emergent bilinguals.* New York, NY: Campaign for Educational Equity (Teachers College).

Gay, G. (2010). Culturally responsive teaching: Theory, research, and practice. New York, NY: Teachers College Press.

Goodman, K. (2006). A critical review of DIBELS. In K. Goodman (Ed.), *The truth about DIBELS: What it is-what it does* (pp. 1–39). Portsmouth, NH: Heinmann.

Gorski, P. (2012). Perceiving the problem of poverty and schooling: Deconstructing the class stereotypes that mis-shape education practice and policy. *Equity and Excellence in Education, 45*(2), 302–319.

Gort, M., & Bauer, E. B. (2012). Holistic approaches to bilingual/biliteracy development, instruction, and research. In E. B. Bauer & M. Gort (Eds.), *Early biliteracy development* (pp. 1–8). New York, NY: Routledge.

Graue, M. E. (1993). *Ready for what? Constructing meanings of readiness for kindergarten.* Albany, NY: State University of New York Press.

Guthrie, J. T., Wigfield, A., & You, W. (2012). Instructional contexts for engagement and achievement in reading. In S. L. Christenson, A. L. Reschly, & C. Wylie (Eds.), *Handbook of research on student engagement* (pp. 601–633). New York, NY: Springer.

Haberman, M. (1991). The pedagogy of poverty versus good teaching. *The Phi Delta Kappan, 73*(4), 290–294.

Haertel, E., & Herman, J.A. (2005). *A historical perspective on validity arguments for accountability testing.* Los Angeles, CA: Center for Research on Evaluation, Standards, and Student Testing.

Hanchon, T., & Allen, R. A. (2013). Identifying students with emotional disturbances: School psychologists' practices and perceptions. *Psychology in the Schools, 50*(2), 193–208.

Hansen, D., Bernstorf, E., & Stuber, G. M. (2004). *The music and literacy connection.* Lanham, MD: Rowman & Littlefield Publishing Group.

Harris, T., & Hodges, R. E. (1995). *The literacy dictionary.* Newark, DE: International Reading Association.

Hart, B., & Risley, T. R. (2003). The early catastrophe: The 30 million word gap. *American Educator, 27*(1), 4–9.

Heath, S. (1983). *Ways with words: Language, life, and work in communities and classrooms.* Cambridge, England: Cambridge University Press.

Hehir, R. (2005). *New directions in special education: Eliminating ableism in policy and practice.* Cambridge, MA: Harvard Education Press.

Helman, L. (2012). *Literacy instruction in multilingual classrooms: Engaging English language learners in elementary school.* New York, NY: Teachers College Press.

Henderson, B. (2011). *The blind advantage: How going blind made me a stronger principal and how including children with disabilities made our school better for everyone.* Cambridge, MA: Havard Education Press.

Hibel, J., Farkas, G., & Morgan, P. L. (2010). Who is placed into special education? *Sociology of Education, 83*(4), 312–332.

Hiebert, E. (Ed.). (2009). *Reading more, reading better: Solving the problems in the teaching of literacy.* New York, NY: The Guilford Press.

Hollo, A., Wehby, J. H., & Oliver, R. M. (2014). Unidentified langauge deficits in children with emotional and behavioral disorders: A meta-analysis. *Exceptional Children, 80*(2), 169–186.

Houk, F. (2005). *Supporting English language learners.* Portsmouth, NH: Heinemann.

Howe, R., & Covell, K. (2013). *Education in the best interests of the child: A children's rights perspective on closing the achievement gap.* Toronto, Canada: University of Toronto Press.

International Reading Association. (2002). *What is evidence-based reading instruction? A position statement.* Newark, DE: International Reading Association.

International Reading Association. (2006). Current issues in special education and reading instruction. *Reading Research Quarterly, 41*(1), 92–93.

Jenkins, J. R., Hudson, R. F., & Johnson, E. S. (2007). Screening for at-risk readers in a response to intervention framework. *School Psychology Review, 36*(4), 582–600.

Johnson, D. (1995). Dyslexia. In T. Harris, & R. E. Hodges (Eds.), *The literacy dictionary* (pp. 64–64). Newark, DE: International Reading Association.

Johnson, E. S., Jenkins, J. R., & Petscher, Y. (2010). Improving the accuracy of a direct route screening process. *Assessment for Effective Intervention, 35*(3), 131–140.

Johnston, P. H. (2004). *Choice words: How our langauge affects children's learning.* Portland, ME: Stenhouse Publishers.

Jones, P., White, J. M., Fauske, J. R., & Carr, J. F. (2011). Creating inclusive schools. In P. Jones, J. R. Fauske, & J. F. Carr (Eds.), *Leading for inclusion: How schools can build on the strengths of all learners.* New York, NY: Teachers College Press.

Kavale, K. A., Spaulding, L. S. & Beam, A. P. (2009). A time to define: Making the specific learning disability definition prescribe specific learning disabilities. *Learning Disability Quarterly, 32*(1), 39–48.

Keogh, B. (2007). Celebrating PL 94-142: The education of all handicapped children act of 1975. *Issues in Teacher Education , 16*(2), 65–69.

Kim, J. (2008). Research and the reading wars. *The Phi Delta Kappan , 89*(5), 372–375.

Klingner, J. K., Almanza de Schonewise, E., Onis, C., & Barletta, L. M. (2008). Misconceptions about the second language acquisition process. In J. K. Klingner, J. J. Hoover, & L. M. Baca (Eds.), *Why do English language learners struggle with reading? Distinguishing language acquisition from learning disabilities* (pp. 17–35). Thousand Oaks, CA: Corwin Press.

Klingner, J. K. (2014). *Why do English language learners struggle with reading? Distinguishing language acquisition from learning disabilities.* NewYork, NY: New York Department of Education.

Koretz, D. M. (2008). *Measuring up.* Cambridge, MA: Harvard University Press.

Law, J., Tomblin, J. B., & Zhang, X. (2008). Characterizing the growth trajectories of langauge-impaired children between 7 and 11 years of age. *Journal of Speech, Langauge, and Hearing Research, 51*, 739–749.

Lazar, A. E., Edwards, P. A., & McMillon, G. T. (2012). *Bridging literacy and equity.* New York, NY: Teachers College Press.

Lippman, L., Burns, S., & McArthur, E. (1996). *Urban schools: The challenge of location and poverty (NCES 96-184).* Washington DC: U.S. Department of Education.

Lipson, M. Y., Chomsky-Higgins, P., & Kanfer, J. (2011). Diagnosis: The missing ingredient in RTI assessment. *The Reading Teacher, 65*(3), 204–208.

Loewen, J. W. (2007). *Lies my teacher told me: Everything your American history textbook got wrong.* New York, NY: Touchstone.

Losen, D. J., & Martinez, T. (2013). *Out of school and off track: The overuse of suspensions in American middle and high schools.* Los Angeles, CA: The Center for Civil Rights Remedies.

MacMillan, D. L. & Siperstein, G. N. (2002). Learning disabilities as operationally defined by schools. In R. D. Bradley, L. Danielson, & D. P. Hallahan (Eds.), *Identification of learning disabilities: Research to practice.* Mahwah, NJ: Erlbaum.

Maggio, V., Granana, N. E., Richaudeau, A., Torres, S., Giannotti, A., & Suburo, A. M. (2014). Behavior problems in children with specific language impairment. *Journal of Child Neurology, 29*(2), 194–202.

Martin Luther King Junior Elementary School Children v. Ann Arbor School District (1979).

Miles, S., & Stipek, D. (2006). Contemporaneous and longitudinal associations between social behavior and literacy achievement in a sample of low-income elementary school children. *Child Development, 77*(1), 103–117.

Milner, H. R. (2010). *Start where you are but don't stay there: Understanding diversity, opportunity gaps, and teaching in today's classrooms.* Cambridge, MA: Harvard Education Press.

Milner, H. R. (2011). Five easy ways to connect with students. *Harvard Education Letter, 27*(1).

Minority Student Achievement Network. (2014). *Overview and Mission.* Available at http://msan.wceruw.org/about/index.html

Morrow, L. M., Paratore, J., Gaber, D., Harrison, C., & Tracey, D. (1993). Family literacy: Perspective and practices. *The Reading Teacher, 47*(3), 194–200.

Mulligan, G. M., Hastedt, S., & Carlivati McCarroll, J. (2012). *First-time kindergarteners in 2010–11: First findings from the kindergarten rounds of early childhood longitudinal study.* Washington, DC: National Center for Education Statistics.

National Assessment of Adult Literacy. (2013a). *Digest of Education Statistics.* Table 398. Literacy skills of adults, by type of literacy, proficiency levels, and selected characteristics: 1992 and 2003. Available at http://nces.ed.gov/programs/digest/d11/tables/dt11_398.asp

National Assessment of Adult Literacy. (2013b). *National Center for Education Statistics*. Available at http://nces.ed.gov/naal/lit_history.asp

National Assessment of Educational Progress. (2014). *The nation's report card*. National Center for Education Statistics. Alexandria, VA: U.S. Department of Education.

National Association for the Education of Young Children. (1995). *Position statement on school readiness*. Washington, DC: National Association for the Education of Young Children.

National Association of the Deaf. (2014). *What is American Sign Language?* Available at http://nad.org/print/issues/american-sign-language/what-is-asl

National Association of School Psychologists. (2007). *Truth in labeling: Disproportionality in special education*. Washington DC: National Education Association.

National Center for Education Statistics. (2010, January 1). *Fast dact: Students with disabilities*. Available at http://nces.ed.gov/fastfacts/display.asp?id=64

National Center for Education Statistics. (2013). *The nation's report card*. Reading 2013: National Assessment of Educational Progress at grades 4 and 8. Available at http://nationsreportcard.gov/reading_math_2013/#/student-groups

National Center for Education Statistics. (2014a). *The condition of education*. Children and Youth with Disabilities. Available at http://nces.ed.gov/programs/coe/indicator_cgg.asp

National Center for Education Statistics. (2014b). *Digest of education statistics*. Number and percentage distribution of teachers in public and private elementary and secondary schools, by selected teacher characteristics: Selected years, 1987–88 through 2011–12. Available at http://nces.ed.gov/programs/digest/d13/tables/dt13_209.10.asp

National Center for Education Statistics. (2014c). *Digest of education statistics*. Number and Percentage of Public School Students Participating in Programs for English Language Learners, Years 2002–03 through 2011–12. Available at http://nces.ed.gov/programs/digest/d13/tables/dt13_204 .20.asp

National Center on Universal Design for Learning. (2014). *National Center on Universal Design for Learning*. The Three Principles of UDL. Available at http://www.udlcenter.org/aboutudl/whatisudl/3principle

National Council of Teachers of English. (2009). Literacy learning in the 21st century: A policy brief produced by the National Council of Teachers of English. Urbana, IL: National Council of Teachers of English.

National Early Literacy Panel. (2009). *Developing early literacy: A report of the National Early Literacy Panel*. Jessup, MD: National Institute for Literacy.

National Education Goals Panel. (1990). *Building a nation of learners*. Available at http://govinfo.library.unt.edu/negp/page3.htm

Neuman, S. B., Copple, C., & Bredekamp, S. (2000). *Learning to read and write: Developmentally appropriate practices for young children*. Washington, DC: National Association for the Education of Young Children.

Nickse, R. (1989). The noises of literacy: An overview of intergenerational and family literacy programs. Washington, DC: Office of Educational Research and Improvement.

Noguera, P. (2008). *The trouble with black boys: And other reflections on race, equity, and the future of public education.* San Francisco, CA: Jossey-Bass.

O'Connell, M. E., Boat, T., & Warner, K. E. (2009). *Preventing mental, emotional, and behavioral disorders among young people.* Washington, DC: The National Academies Press.

Office of Civil Rights. (2012, March 6). *U.S. Department of Education.* New Data from U.S. Department of Education Highlights Educational Inequities. Available at http://www.ed.gov/news/press-releases/new-data-us-department-education-highlights-educational-inequities-around-teache

Pearson, D. (2004). The reading wars. *Educational Policy, 18,* 216–252.

Pearson, D. (2006). Forward. In K. Goodman (Ed.), *The truth about DIBELS: What it is- what it does* (pp. v–xix). Portsmouth, NH: Heinemann.

Pinker, S. (1997). Foreword. In D. McGuinness (Ed.), *Why our children can't read and what we can do about it: A scientific revolution in reading* (pp. ix–x). New York: NY: Simon & Schuster.

Ramsey, P. (2004). *Teaching and learning in a diverse world: Multicultural education for young children (3rd ed.).* New York, NY: Teachers College Press.

Ravitch, D. (2011). *The death and life of the great American school system: How testing and choice are undermining education.* New York, NY: Basic Books.

Redfield, S., & Kraft, T. (2012). What color is special education? *Journal of Law and Education, 41,* 129.

Reid, D., & Valle, J. W. (2004). The discursive practice of learning disability: Implications for instruction and parent-school relations. *Journal of Learning Disabilities, 37*(6), 466–481.

Reynolds, C. R., & Shaywitz, S. E. (2009). Response to internvention: Ready or not? Or, from wait-to-fail to watch-them-fail. *School Psychology Quarterly, 24*(2), 130–145.

Risko, V. J., & Walker-Dalhouse, D. (2012). *Be that teacher! Breaking the cycle for struggling readers.* New York, NY: Teachers College Press.

Routman, R. (1988). *Transitions from literature to literacy.* Portsmouth, NH: Heinemann.

Schnorr, R. (2011). Intensive reading instruction for learners with developmental disabililites. *The Reading Teacher, 65*(1), 35–45.

Scott, D. (1997). *Contempt and pity: Social policy and the image of the damaged black psyche, 1880–1996.* Chapel Hill, NC: The University of North Carolina Press.

Sendak, M. (1963). *Where the wild things are.* New York: Harper & Row.

Shanahan, T., & Beck, I. (2006). Effective literacy teaching for English-language learners. In D. August & T. Shanahan (Eds.), *Developing literacy in second- language learners: Report of the national literacy panel on language-minority children and youth* (pp. 415–488). Mahwah, NJ: Lawrence Erlbaum Associates.

Shea, M. (2012). *Running records: Authentic instruction in early childhood education.* New York, NY: Routledge.

Shepard, D. (2001). Portuguese speakers. In M. Swan & B. Smith (Eds.), *Learner English: A teacher's guide to interference and other problems* (pp. 113–128). New York, NY: Cambridge University Press.

Shepard, L. H. (2009). *Standards, assessment, and accountability: Education policy white paper.* National Academy of Education. Washington, DC: National Academy of Education.

Singleton, G. (2013). *More courageous conversations about race.* Thousand Oaks, CA: Corwin.

Singleton, G., & Linton, C. W. (2006). *Courageous conversations about race: A field guide for achieving equity in schools.* Thousand Oaks, CA: Corwin.

Smitherman, G. (2002). Toward a national public policy on langauge. In L. Delpit (Ed.), *The skin that we speak* (pp. 163–178). New York, NY: The New Press.

Snow, C. B. (1998). *Preventing reading difficulties in young children.* Washington, DC: National Academy of Sciences-National Research Council.

Stiggins, R., & Chappuis, J. (2006). What a difference a word makes: Assessment FOR learning rather than assessment OF learning helps students succeed. *Journal of Staff Development, 27*(1), 10–14.

Stipek, D., Newton, S., & Chudgar, A. (2010). Learning-related behaviors and literacy achievement in elementary school-aged children. *Early Childhood Research Quarterly, 25,* 385–395.

Stoughton, E. (2006). Marcus and Harriet: Living on the edge in school and society. In E. A. Brantlinger (Ed.), *Who benefits from special education? Remediating (fixing) other people's children* (pp. 145–163). Mahwah, NJ: Lawrence Erlbaum Associates.

Strickland, D., & Morrow, L. M. (Eds.). (1989). *Emerging literacy: Young children learn to read and write.* Newark, DE: International Reading Association.

Stubbs, M. (2002). Some basic sociolinguistic concepts. In L. Delpit (Ed.), *The skin that we speak* (pp. 63–85). New York, NY: The New Press.

Sullivan, A.L., & Field, S. (2013). *Does special education improve preschoolers' academic skills?* Charlottesville: University of Virginia, National Center for Research on Early Childhood Education.

Sulzby, E. (1985). Children's emergent reading of favorite storybooks: A developmental study. *Reading Research Quarterly, 20*(4), 458–481.

Sulzby, E. (1996). Roles of oral and written language as children approach conventional literacy. In C. Pontecorvo, M. Orsolini, B. Burge, & L. Resnick (Eds.), *Children's early text construction* (pp. 25–46). Mahwah, NJ Lawrence Erlbaum Associates.

Sutherland, K. S., & Morgan, P. L. (2003). Implications of transcational processes in classrooms for students with emotional/behavioral disorders. *Preventing School Failure: Alternative Education for Children and Youth, 48*(1), 32–37.

Tatum, B. D. (1997). *"Why are all the Black kids sitting together in the cafeteria?": And other conversations about race.* New York, NY: Basic Books.

Taylor, D., & Dorsey-Gaines, C. (1988). *Growing up literate: Learning from inner city families.* Portsmouth, NH: Heinemann.

Thurlow, M. L., Quenemoen, R. F., & Lazarus, S. S. (2013). *Meeting the needs of special education students: Recommendations for the race to the top consorita and states.* Minneapolis, MN: National Center on Educational Outcomes.

Tollefson, J. W. (2013). Critical issues in language policy in education. In J. Tollefson, *Language policy in education: Critical issues* (pp. 3–10). New York, NY: Routledge.

Townsend, B. (2000). The disproportionate discipline of African American learners: Reducing school suspension and expulsions. *Exceptional Children, 66*(3), 381–391.

Tummer, W., & Greaney, K. (2010). Defining dyslexia. *Journal of Learning Disabilities, 43*(3), 229–243.

United Nations Educational, Scientific, and Cultural Organization. (1994). *Salamanca statement.* Salamanca, Spain: United Nations Educational, Scientific, and Cultural Organization.

United Nations Educational, Scientific and Cultural Organization. (2004). *The plurality of literacy and its implications for policies and programmes.* Paris, France: United Nations Educational, Scientific and Cultural Organization.

United Nations Educational, Scientific and Cultural Organization. (2009). *Policy guidelines on inclusion in education.* Paris, France: United Nations Educational, Scientific and Cultural Organization.

U.S. Department of Education. (2006a). *Topic: Identification of learning disabilities.* Available at http://idea.ed.gov/explore/view/p/,root,dynamic,TopicalBrief,23,

U.S. Department of Education. (2006b). Topic: Individualized Education Program (IEP), Team Meetings and Changes to the IEP. Available at http://idea.ed.gov/explore/view/p/,root,dynamic,TopicalBrief,9,

U.S. Department of Education. (2010). *Free appropriate public education under Section 504* . Available at http://www2.ed.gov/about/offices/list/ocr/docs/edlite-FAPE504.html

U.S. Department of Education. (2013). *National Assessment of Educational Progress (NAEP).* Institute of Education Sciences, National Center for Education Statistics. Washington, DC: National Center for Education Statistics.

U.S. Department of Education. (2014). Regulations: Part 300/A/300.8/c/10. http://idea.ed.gov/explore/view/p/%2Croot%2Cregs%2C300%2CA%2C300%252E8%2Cc%2C10%2C

Valencia, R. R. (1997). Conceptualizing the notion of deficit thinking. In R. R. Valencia (Ed), *The evolution of deficit thinking: Educational thought and practice. The Standford series on education and public policy* (pp. 1–12). Bristol, PA: Falmer Press.

Valencia, S. W., Smith, A. T., Reece, A. M., Li, M., Wixon, K. K., & Newman, H. (2010). Oral reading fluency assessment: Issues of construct, criterion, and consequential validity. *Reading Research Quarterly, 45*(3), 270–291.

Valli, C., & Lucas, C. (2000). *Linguistics of American sign language: An introduction.* Washington, DC: Gallaudet University Press.

Venezky, R. L. (1995). Literacy. In T. L. Harris & R. E. Hodges (Eds.), *The literacy dictionary* (p. 142). Newark, DE: International Reading Association.

Venezky, R. L., Wagner, D. A., & Cilberti, B. S. (1990). *Toward defining literacy.* Newark, DE: International Reading Association.

Viorst, J. (1972). *Alexander and the terrible, horrible, no good, very bad day.* New York, NY: Simon & Schuster.

Vlach, S., & Burcie, J. (2010). Narratives of the struggling reader. *The Reading Teacher, 63*(6), 522–525.

Waldron, T. R. (2004). *Working hard, falling short: America's working families and the pursuit of economic security.* Chevy Chase, MD: Working Poor Families Project.

Walmsley, S. A., & Allington, R. L. (1995). Redefining and reforming instructional support programs for at-risk students. In R. L. Allington & S. A. Walmsley (Eds.), *No quick fix: Rethinking literacy programs in America's elementary schools* (pp. 19–44). New York, NY: Teachers College Press.

Wei, X, Blackorby, J., & Schiller, E. (2011). Growth in reading achievement of students with disabilities, ages 7 to 17. *Exceptional Children, 78*(1), 89–106.

Wiley, T. (2005). Ebonics: Background to the policy debate. In D. Ramirez, T. Wiley, G. deKlerk, E. Lee, & W. Wright (Eds.), *Ebonics: The urban education debate* (pp. 3–17). Tonawanda, NY: Multilingual Matters Limited.

Williams, J. (1995). Phonemic awareness. In T. L. Harris & R. E. Hodges (Eds.), *The literacy dictionary* (pp. 185–186). Newark, DE: International Reading Association.

Wixson, K. K., & Valencia, S. W. (2011). Assessment in RTI: What teachers and specialists need to know. *The Reading Teacher, 64*(6), 466–469.

Wolf, M. (2007). *Proust and the squid: The story and science of the reading brain.* New York, NY: HarperCollins Publishers.

Yell, M. L., Rogers, D., & Rogers, E. L. (1988). The legal history of special education: What a long, strange trip it's been! *Remedial and Special Education, 19*(4), 219–228.

Zhang, D., Katsiyannis, A., Ju, S., & Roberts, E. (2014). Minority representation in special education. *Journal of Child and Family Studies, 23*, 118–127.

Zigmond, N. (1993). Learning disabilities from an educational perspective. In G. R. Lyon, D. B. Gray, J. F. Kavanaugh, & N.A. Kraznegor (Eds.), *Better understanding learning disabilities: New views from research and their implications for education and public policies* (pp. 251–272). Baltimore, MD: Paul H. Brookes.

Index

About the Author

Deborah L. Wolter is an elementary teacher consultant in Ann Arbor Michigan public schools. She has worked for over 18 years with public school teachers and their students from all walks of life (including those in special education, Title I, response to intervention, and English language learners) and who were in different places of exploring multiple languages and literacies. Prior to that, she worked as an early childhood education teacher for 10 years. Deborah completed a BA degree in early childhood and elementary education and an MA degree in reading from Eastern Michigan University. She also completed an additional endorsement in learning disabilities from Madonna University. Visit her website at readingupsidedown. wordpress.com.